PETALS

BIJAYANANDA MISHRA

Clever Fox®
PUBLISHING
Chennai • Bangalore

CLEVER FOX PUBLISHING
Chennai, India

Published by CLEVER FOX PUBLISHING 2023

ISBN: 978-93-56488-91-5

ABOUT THE AUTHOR

Sri Bijayananda Mishra lives in Cuttack City of Orissa, India. He was born in Keonjhar town in 1951 and grew up in Puri, the beach city of Orissa. He completed his graduation in Engineering, Electronics, and telecommunication in 1977. And post-graduation in Computer Engineering Data Processing in 1988. His professional life was as a telecommunication engineer in the then Orissa State Electricity Board at Talcher Thermal Plant. After post-graduation, he opted for a career in his state for computerization and networking.

In the last four years before retirement, he completed the project of core banking for 17 district co-operative banks and state co-operative banks. And with a central data center and networking for the banks and their branches in the state. In his retired life, after 2014, his passion is meditation and writing. 2016, the author faced brain injury by falling unconsciously. He survived but had no coordination part of the memory. But in 2018, he recovered well but was confined to his residence. His only passion is writing poems (English) and other topics. His love for spirituality and friendship. The Book PETALS is his first attempt into the writer's world. Age 72. Birthday 10th February 1951. His mother tongue is Oriya. He is fluent in English and Hindi.

Bijayananda Mishra

I dedicate the Book PETAL, of English poetry at the lotus feet of my mother Mrs. Padmavati Mishra 90. This is my first attempt but she was the first teacher, mentor, guide and inspiration for my life.

Bijayananda Mishra

GRATITUDE

I thank my wife Mrs. Ranjita Mishra for her immense support and constant inspiration to write. Had not she showed immense interest to complete this book would not have been possible. I express indebted to my son, Advocate, Sri Swayambhu Mishra for his immense interest towards publishing my first book.

Bijayananda Mishra

PROLOGUE

The English poems I have written are only capsules to include contemporary society and the continuing conflict of human nature with the parabolic generation shift. I prefer describing changing times, the landscape, customs, habits, and reformation through practices. Love emphasizes human love, kindness, and sympathy, the soft part of human existence. Many poems highlight child education, women's empowerment, and literacy drive cleanness for bright aspects of human life. I never forgot to focus on nature and earth, critical factors for preservation and rebuilding destroyed forest land and disturbed climate. The first attempt at my poems while reshaping to a book, PETALS, is mostly 60 lines, approximately 300 words each. Each poem is based on the above mentioned issues or ensuing current events. I shall never fail to express my gratitude to Google, Facebook, Cambridge Dictionary, and Spell-checker for the best helpful cyberspace online services. Without countless information through Google Search and English meanings for words through the Cambridge Dictionary online service, I feel it would not be possible to write on varied topics with the right words. The Spell Checker helped with typing errors that could not have been eliminated and corrected. I remember the constant inspiration of Mrs. Shinaya Ali, Pakistan, and Mrs. Gertrud Resch, Austria. And many poet friends on Facebook. Their observation messages have given me enough courage to write this book.

Bijayananda Mishra

CONTENTS

A Birthday

Probe life amazingly complex,
Myriads of hope desire index,
Born with no golden spoon,
Birth in a family poor distinct,

Human never chooses wombs,
The creator plays nicely unknown,
Accept birth later understood,
Succumb to reality, adjust well,

Abject poverty a curse enumerate,
The list of suffering pain is longer,
Hunger is perennial without food,
A thatched cottage, mud-walled,

Bamboo and paddy straws roof,
Sleep on a straw mattress, teenage,
In one room, parents, children sleep,
At night moon shines through the roof,

The room is lighted by sun percolates,
If Lord deprived us, siblings sad,
Crumpled our teenage dreams,
Burning utter hope reminds me today,

How much struggle in life but faced,
Successful in studies career found,
Inroad for wealth and fame opened,
Obscure unknown rustic boy no more,

A respected officer with attendants,
A few vehicles, driver, bungalow,
Furnished as life changed luxurious,
Parents with me, brother, sisters,

Relatives scantily recognized us, visiting,
Had in due course family children,
Birthday never could know to celebrate,
Wide circles of friends, kin, neighbor,

Converging gleefully to my residence,
The cake, icing sugar inscribed,
Happy Birthday and name candle lit,
Extinguish the flames instantly matched,

Loud claps praised showered happily,
Every year the moments I hide feelings,
Lived not with cakes but without rice,
This life is decorated with dress positions,

My wife knows me, my heart, holds my hand,
Fight my tears not to embarrass guests,
Not to disturb my children, parents,
The day, with a fine dinner, goodwill,

The man living in this frame remembers,
Wanted to celebrate a birthday alone,
Chance I got to meet a child on the street,
Playing with cycle tire torn clothes,

I thought he was my childhood starkly,
Called him to the footpath and sat together,
He was hungry has not eaten for a day,
Visited his home small hut under a tree,

Arranged groceries, cooked prepared dishes,
The child, his parents his siblings enjoyed,
The aromas touched me to reminisce,
I Jovially revealed my birthday to them,

The whole lot was happy, smiling, noisy,
We sat together on the ground, had lunch,
Sumptuous meal tasty the woman cooked,
Worth watching children's happiness,

Confide a birthday so happy grooved,
Their glittering eyes, smiles etched,
Waited for that day, guest my family missed me,
Passed that day with the child, his siblings,

Back home late at night intimated to my wife,
Understood, she hugged and wished me,
A birthday was a different heart celebrated.

A Grace In Desolation

In desert sand dunes, cactus thorn blooms,
In placid lakes, lotus in mud look sun at noon,
Rocky mountain slopes bush blossom pink,
Nature, incredible places, in love, if ever wink!

In the hot summer, I found myself in a land, desolate,
Dry grass, rocks, no greens, in shades, locate,
Tired too, sat reclined on a small tree and took a rest,
Distant mountains, blue skies, clouds, if the best,

Sank in deep thought in solitude, mysterious,
Felt blue skies sun alone blaze earth curious,
Kiss it at horizons east n west orange ball,
A sink in dark skies, stars twinkle if wink all,

A bright moon rises all alone, smiles stars in tears,
Cold dawn, in sun rays, red flowers, dew wear,
Jewel in rocky fields in bed nature wake n yawn,
Mind travel blue ocean eyes lost deep bottom,

Dark if bed water atop sunlight does glisten,
Lone pearl so bright if moon in dark skies,
Marine lives milling twinkle as stars shine,
Incredible poem nature writes all in grace,

Look with so sleepy saw own creations trace,
Shrink in fear of own kind, so cruel blind greedy,
Epic cover in war blood soaked lust needy,
Amazed in millions, a lone soul shines bright,

Ablaze with love, care, and compassion serve at sight,
Revelation did happen in the dark ages alone,
In cycles, bloom realized, spread wisdom,
The limitless expanse of sand green no basis,

An island of paradise, greens water in an oasis,
In sorrows, heart sink alone Bapu in billion,
A stick in hand cloths cover met all in the nation,
So infectious his smile, innocence in bloom,

Silence, nonviolence, rejection, untruth, swoon,
Country in darkness saw the light of freedom,
If the tribute nation paid death in hatred n venom,
Returned home quiet flash solitude one bloom,

From a lone red flower in rubble Bapu in a cocoon,
Felt all systems in the act, I wish, lonely breath to live,
From womb till death only in action, a life do weave,
Slept deep saw dream ancient n past canvas drawn,

A million insects bite alone honey bee drink in blossom,
When nature witnesses time unravel canvas fearsome,
Splendid in beauty ushers a grace in desolation.

A Nervous Wreck

A facet of family life

Lose once ravishing style,
Entices a beautiful smile,
Fare beauty charm invite,
Exhibits goods costs bite,
Tempt heart buy car new,
A family urge for a flat due,
Kids cajole vacation travel,
Asset new model n mobile,
Agree instantly and imbecile,
Remind income to a break,
Find now a nervous wreck, (1)

A facet of service life

Urban life cost n demand,
Frying pan to fire if I land,
Heart demand moon grab,
Loan payments often barb,
Happy life, sorrows greet,
Equanimity income meet,

Bolt from blue it transfer,
Reveal my pathos I suffer,
Staff, colleagues, boss mute,
A nervous wreck fate brute, (2)

A facet of retired life

It is true to me but is a lie to all,
Life is torture if it enthralls,
She laughs, he taunts jokes,
People look in awe n mock,
Make home breaks life tell,
Fallen from heaven to hell,
Retire from job now a village,
Alone a couple got ripe age,
On rare occasions, visit to illness,
No doctor medical distress,
Get peace bliss up to the neck,
Happy, not a nervous wreck, (3)

Hazard of environment

Watch leisure news live,
Corona sick medic beehive,
Election news Pandora box,
Procession rallies voter fox,
Lockdown, vaccine in force,
Strike violence and, of course,
Witness village amid nature,
Summer heat dries verdure,

River sandy bed ponds dry,
Sweltering hot wind limb fry,
Awake a good time surmise,
Time will heal mirth, precise,
Ushers rain earth aromatic wet,
Peasant in field green velvet,
Let monsoon rain late break,
A farmer is a nervous wreck (4)

Hope clue to uncertain future

Life struggles, to me, the world,
Rare, presume happy emerald,
Sadness, pain, and misery reason,
Sweetens peace, joy, and health often,
In life, experience a testing time,
Bitter thought, time, later refine,
Never lose hope, heaven's sake,
Repent, find me a nervous wreck (5)

A Night Nostalgic

A service life just got alive in me,
Young from Alma Mater as an engineer,
Butterflies in the heart, rainbows in a young mind,
A dream enwrapped for a career, a rosy future,

No girlfriend predated least a green valley,
Aspiring heart limitless, fruits of books,
The night lamp, books, digesting knowledge,
Technologies of electronics, telecommunication,

Digital information technology understanding,
Float songs of Bollywood of the seventies,
Out of the hostel to the lonely nights, humming,
Soaked in love for a time so young a mind,

Thrills in a cool breeze, eyes lost in the void,
Overwhelmed heart with a surreal inner joy,
Solitude intoxicating from thickness,
Thickness as intricate technology,

Mind looked up at the study table sharply, hammer,
A probing mind, intelligence, intuition,

The fatigue, from the hostel room to a lake,
Tranquil silvery lake lights of a night sky,

Passed days dreamy few times dawn breaks,
A night came in life service life took root,
A rented house, few belongings, hard work,
A cook served dinner full moon night,

Gentle breeze, bright night sky so alluring,
Got up so late, world asleep, an unreal world, lonely,
Dark houses, empty streets, stray dogs barking,
In the night, never knew why roamed aimless,

The mind swirling thoughts, least understood,
Nostalgic nightly prowl from campus near the lake,
Gone the student life, gone these books, classes,
Dreams of a young heart slowly maturing,

Meticulous planning, overseas opportunities,
One night a railway track silvery on a full moon,
A cement culvert at the rail track sat cool alone,
A train passed fast, tearing silent night,

Lighted windows deem, time sleeping in darkness,
Silence reigned silver night cool a gentle breeze,
Sat for an hour or more, felt so lonely,
Tears unchecked why for leaving home,

Night train to an unknown destination, people,
Why do I seek to quit family, luxury in an alien land,
Life will end, a career will conclude, life in the evening,
The night cast a lonely night, the moon shining,

Knew the moon to sink into the horizon, surely,
A new day the dawn misses the moon star hidden,
Birds chirping in ecstasy, no known faces,
Why obliterate name fame unnoticed a day...

None to shed a tear, to remember me in a foreign land,
Why not my place, be a small job, kill an aspiring heart,
A budding engineer serving his own soil for life,
The people, known eyes, known smiles,

So surreal, why O' engineer crying as a lone wolf,
Come with us pass your life, be like us,
Heard I was crying, a track of rail had dews,
No more I found the silvery night a lonely, silent,

Noises deep within returned early dawn,
The moon was a ghost, pale and sad,
Whispered to me, O' spirit, happiness is wealth,
Happiness when eyes will be closing, never to open,

Not a lonely departure as this lonely night,
All will be around me, to cry tears running down,
I could never know, so happy and in smiles!!!
A night ever nostalgic in life hunts in love.

A Pendant

A human sees a future bleak time,
Few say apocalyptic to erase fine,
Prediction of virus cleans species,
Doomsday on climate nature perish,

Fiction forecast human settles in space,
Underwater cities, human survival a grace,
The hope, natural regain balance hunts,
Healthy human life growth on all fronts,

New millennium dark phase to clear,
A century on an anvil waits for discovery near,
A century ago was dark fear fever toil,
Innovation unknown transforms soil,

Poverty diminishes, lifetime rise visible,
Generation attitude, desire admirable,
Female fantasy her necklace in place,
A pendant shines bright in her grace,

Little pendant is the trust of omen good,
Modern women believe pendant stood,
Credence to secure life in pain, worry,
Pendant augurs protection, lacking sorry,

Rich, poor, tribal, all faith and place,
Pendant is simple to trust divine blesses,
A tiny locket to a necklace, gold or beads,
A pendant is an inscription of divine creed,

Ram, Krishna, Siva, Sakti, Anjaneya,
Sai, thousands of gods picture enjoy,
Symbols, Om, Cross, geometric shape,
Letter of Sacred books pendant trace,

The human mind lives in faith, gets courage,
Little pendant to even child or in age,
Men wear pendants considered sacred,
A thread or chain with pendant lead,

Round an arm left-or-right stays tight,
Believes most, it protects life right,
Amazing, humans still trust the unknown,
Erases fear, cools mind, saves often,

Magical effect on human heart shine,
Pendant with male or female saves, fine,
Fire ceremony, worship, and prayer a lot,
Pendant born in an occasion, share most,

A Pendant

Human prays with beads in a string,
A pendant in joint, in whisper rolls, swing,
Incredible mystery, the world over a sight,
The human mind utters a name to bead delight,

A touch on the pendant felt like a boon to life,
Each cycle touch a million faith is bright.
The pendant is a mighty symbol of trust n faith,
Centuries glitter with silver, gold for wealth.

A Renegade

Rise of the leader

The advent of youth mix mainstream,
Social fiber rejuvenates, in essence, wins,
Win flamboyance service immaculate,
Crystal clear speech nicely promulgates,

Influence people talks in fire n fume,
Eminence on, rise as a leader, right tune,
Maddening crowd applause roars loud,
Unknown spirit a face impact n proud,

People presume impeccable character,
Their leader is honest hard work clear,
Clever as a crow, selective, wise, choice,
Amass followers, moral policy all rejoice,

Prevent corruption, clean n great vision,
A leader today rules a people, root actions,
A person in need friend indeed does care,
Help people in peril support well share,

Peace, prosperity, progress, people watch,
Worshipped as a benevolent Godly match,
Command over a people, trust the total, party,
The story ends in time rule crumbles empty, (1)

Rejected in life

Behind the trust, treachery grows with greed,
Power affluence position corrodes a creed,
Plunder power-drunk spirit, people a sock,
Ignorant the ruler coteries exploit n mock,

Corruption is a curse on people, erode ethic,
In public life, the clean image turns dirty and pathetic,
Bribe, cheat, siphon public property, loot,
Empty treasury, the law, rule under the boot,

Collapse system people betrayed in anger,
Yesterday, mighty at road sweeps beggar,
Disenchanted followers today hackle ruler,
Reverently plead to rise again, grab clever,

Grab power position rule again leader miss,
Lifelong soul serves, loved people, fate kiss,
Hurt, people look down today, ruler guess,
Adopt, resign from public life, quit a mess,

Wise a chosen reclusion, the past will not invade,
Unknown insignificant life silent no tirade,
Erase repentance, overlooked once brigade,
No tear, pain, dried, remember a renegade, (2)

Discovers a recluse

Happy today with new chapter nature laps,
Family, the friend, known forgot total perhaps,
A friend is a bird, animal, or plant whispers to entice,
Pure O soul love nature get simple practice,

A fresh breeze will refresh a mind, satiate brook,
Meadows allow you to sleep in bed soft to hook,
Tree shade will be your shelter fruit nourish,
Bird chirping leaf flutter brook murmur wish,

Wish O soul, forget unreal reel in motion all,
Our music is eternal listen to wind n enthrall,
A nostalgic feel world unknown once came slowly,
Transient power wealth age fame not gold glow,
Your sojourn means learn creation pervade,
Speechless listens, remembers a renegade, (3)

A Time Obnoxious

Let me tell you, unforgettable love,
It still probes the innermost chambers,
In my heart floats childhood memory,
The cowshed was the best place for fun,

Playing bat and ball, flying kites,
Thatched roof cowshed of mud, straws,
Cows and bullocks were five and a calf,
Passing time, feeding them,

Washing the floor of the cowshed, cleaning cattle,
Funny each recognizes their name,
Responds with moos waving ears,
Looks directly get happy at scrubbing,

Their neck face get caressed, falling eyes,
It was as if causing dozing time,
The calf was our playmate,
Love to jump hopping for a length,

Never leave far from mother cow,
Her name is Gouri, responds to our calling,
Mostly loved cow in the family worshipped,
Her milk, so sweet, still fresh in memory,

Use to remove the rope, tied, and use to sit near,
Scrub her skin, caress her neck flaps,
In solitary moments she enjoys my talk,
Had faith she understood, and if listening,

Harmless, most lovable, Gouri, our life,
She brushes her neck, flaps soft, woolly,
In life, I acquired intricate relationships,
She was our family member, so lovable,

An event that shook us, a baby born to her,
It was a stillbirth dead calf was removed,
The place was cleaned, Gouri was sitting,
The entire evening after school, I was with her,

She was silently crying noticed her tears,
Reluctant to feed on grass, she was still,
Her head was resting on her legs,
I kept my arm on her spine reclined,

These moments of sadness,
Her world if collapsed, and searching for her child,
I understood, felt crying, consoled,
My childish way burbling unending,

If cursed, unseen God is cruel to take away,
Lo found she was licking me on her tongue,
I was wiping her tears evening longest,
Cruel, a time never fled, only torturing us,

It was getting dark, a time obnoxious,
Gouri is no more, yet find twilight years,
In silence, seclusion, hear cow moos,
Hunts a sweet moment, our cow and me,

Shared intimate relations, love, sorrows,
A time obnoxious was etched in rock,
In my memories… floating, many a time.

Aberration Anchor

Gone down in gut instinct,
Born as equal, be free distinct,
Equal to breathe live exist,
Equal right to watch and resist, (1)

Equal, to hear voices speak,
Equal rights, speaking tricks,
Equal, to feed cloth shelter,
Equal, lesson-wise prosper, (2)

Equal, to work, earn means,
Equal is love, hope, dreams,
One race, humans, a species,
Color, class, caste no basis, (3)

Equal before God ever exist,
Equal, to realize Him desist
One world, nation n family,
Rivers meet oceans and simply, (4)

Lifestyle costume n habits,
Faith practice of trust hits,
Colors white, black, brown,
Few ignominy rest renown, (5)

Billion people n languages,
Trillion views differ crazes,
Oceans divide a continent,
Culture, faith, or sentiment, (6)

One world all nations built,
In one country, many families lit,
Born equal n mere a notion,
Real unequally an aberration, (7)

Equals purity, love, kind care,
Equals services to all shares,
Equals human blood a death,
Equal time steals ill, wealth, (viii)

Equals fate fortune luck test,
Equals destiny progress best,
Peace, prosperity, joys equal,
Human nature pure enthrall, (9)

Equal a human race eternal,
Anchor aberration sink total,
Greed, hatred discriminates,
Ego, jealous anger dominates, (10)

Selfish n cruel nature elusive,
Evil choice aberration deceives,
Equal opportunities wash sins,
Equal nobility humility cleans, (11)

Equals devotion surrender win,
Aberration emotion pollutes sin,
Equally, minds are detached, reject lust,
Aberration attaches, tempt worst, (12)

Light burns within light equals,
Aberration willful dark mortals,
Equal inheritance reacts to deeds,
Equal benefit good act indeed, (13)

Equally, punishments for evil actions,
Agony, worry, suffering, aberration,
Equals justice spirits ever meet,
Aberration ruin, innocent neat, (14)

Verses of an aberration anchor,
Human life in sock halt prosper,
Aberration anchors bright future,
Aberration, mistake, equal horror. (15)

Abjure Aspersion

Guilt tortures me, blind to failure,
Adequate plan effort rare secure,
Whimsical instinct struggles hard,
Abysmal estimate snatch reward, (1)

Hope against hope betray, elusive,
Eloquent, thought dream divisive,
Young mind I grow youth temper,
Aggressive often n obstacle suffer, (2)

Epitome entangle sock inferiority,
Fail to digest superior n seniority,
Savage nature cast aspersion nit,
Arrogance, ego, ignorance, rule threat, (3)

Backbones the future generation,
Anarchic mind shame veneration,
Mute society deaf legal machines,
Burn shopping mall, city rhymes, (4)

Insinuate insults humiliate the leader,
Perverse persuasive dilutes order,
Ignore national sentiment respect,
University campus burns inspection, (5)

Disorder disunity disillusion nail,
Mushroom of unemployment failure,
Terror, violence, suicide, state rule,
Clueless leadership parent people, (6)

Amber alerts show red, turn green,
Youth abjure aspersion n screen,
Skill credential credits, courage,
Rebuild life settle family envisage, (7)

Agronomy economy research well,
The vastness of nation nature to quell,
Sympathy social movements serve,
Empathy Covid patient help curve, (viii)

Rise mass youth collaboration hail,
Spread rural field shelter food trail,
Oxygen medicine carries patients all,
Tearful, watch youth cremates, call, (9)

Face dangers to life youth act angel,
Ensure mass vaccination mask fuel,
Young women drive n oxygen freight,
Railroad flight lead with men great, (10)

Horrors of May second wave decline,
Son, daughters of sacred soil do incline,
Salute to bold daredevil future seed,
Motherland days of agony pain need, (11)

Flutter University campus lockdown,
Indwellers commit flag march crown,
Desolate roads bazaar people in fear,
Million-strong youth, prompt secure, (12)

Dedicate my ink golden color cherish,
Abjure aspersion rinse sin n blemish,
Salute people, parents, leaders, heroism,
Youth of nation rebuilds nationalism, (13)

A new dawn, a new decade, holds the mantle,
Today's lad, tomorrow's leader, mettle,
Shelters in retired life, senior citizen,
Abjure aspersion child wiser netizen. (14)

Abjure Segregation

Cactus today myself, my thorn,
Thorn untouchable, the day born,
Abjure, shed a tear, smiles flower,
Born, segregate from all, cower, (1)

Beautiful flowers and garden fence,
Grow inside, root out an offense,
Contemplates, people love roses,
Eloquence n writing poems and prose, (2)

Tolerate a thorn, justly ignore it,
Rose exists in the class I little hit,
The caste class birth look down upon,
Despise affluent aristocracy torn, (3)

Poor life face derivation content,
Cactus I grow desolation decent,
Never find a rose that grows notice,
Perplex me yet, abjure prejudice, (4)

Sprout from soil n equal nature,
Cactus plants decorate my flower,
Incredible insight into myopic detail,
Age-old vices, blind beliefs nail,(5)

Human life n my fluid resembles,
Name, surname, class ensemble,
Watch Creeper Jasmine fragrant,
Creep on your fence face vibrant, (6)

Ornate idol top chest, ascendant,
From very birth, I felt discordant,
O' human creeper needs support,
Delicate-group enjoys all rapport, (7)

Cactus I grow in arid life deprive,
Open to skies, blister sun I revive,
Knows discrimination un-natural,
Lord Grace me succulent enthrall, (viii)

Small bees abjure wall love equal,
Less discriminate rose cactus pal,
Ego-blind people mind the class, color,
Prejudice color, pride, hate inferiority, (9)

Inferior only notion wall you erect,
Constitution, freedoms yet respect,
The Temple door close category persists,
Marriage, relationship group resist, (10)

Ceremony debar caste is sacrilege,
Neither people nor country assuages,
Mute spectators n society are helpless,
Deprivation of self-respect distress, (11)

Dream cactus garden never build,
Part of verdure nature looks yield,
Homogeneous human effort tower,
Mix caste creed race praise shower, (12)

Glass tower glaze bright shines all,
Indwellers mix with class, feel tall,
Part-of-nature humans share a lesson,
Cactus, me schedule caste tribe mourn, (13)

Solemn pledge let us unite a union,
Solemn a pledge abjure, segregation.
Pledge solemnly ask for equality, freedom,
Behold our earth, heaven's kingdom. (14)

Abode

In a tiny village, the calm river kisses grew up a soul.
Midnight lamp burned endlessly future stamp the goal,
Caterpillar of rustic life weaved moments intricate,
The serenity and silence of cottages aspire n fabricate,

Time sweeps off the feet of the spirit to the career farthest,
Remote the paradise of solitude, a bungalow on a hill,
Gentle clouds sail smoothly along the lawn affluent in a thrill,

Distant mountains in a haze stand mysteriously,
Looks in dreamy eyes waves of the blue sea so curios,
Greenfields, small a village, people worth watching them,
The city crowd in a mask enact life amazing and insane,

The mansion and luxurious life twisted minds in fame,
Gazed these spirits, incredible cruelty ravaged nature,
Greed and lust looked away from vanishing features,
Folks of the little village far below the bungalow purest,

Reflections of Divinity, innocence, simplicity in a crest,
In tears felt awakened thoughts, this world that loved more,
The noise of home waves crashing inshore fails to allure,
Far off these hills, own village waits for a reader to hug in love,

Alone in life passionate in greens, blue ravines, loving souls,
Sun was setting down blue skies, felt to stay the rest of the time,
Career fade, dreams did melt, nature in solitude inclined,
Conspicuous hunger for city life, infra was taunting well,

Amid greens, were buried the next day, the soul turned an alien,
Time rolled so fast on wheels ripe age down the hills,
Tiny a cottage, simplicity rules, silence pervades mine,
Union with nature, the divine thoughts sail a cloud,
An abode destiny creates in soft hands.

Accord

Divert the mundane realm, the soul,
Unrealistic aspiration chased a goal,
Mother's death at birth imprinted,
Father at early childhood departed, (1)

Fate assured helpless age provided,
Elder brother, elder to age a decade,
He was his father, mother, or teacher,
Life passed tranquil years immature, (2)

Instilled character, courage, decision,
Guided his lonely life, taught a lesson,
Back at home from work in the evening,
Class notes, study book, his teaching, (3)

Workout problems explaining detail,
Performed high school record to hail,
Watched it, less smiled, hugged tightly,
Surprised found tear inkling slightly, (4)

Caught emotions, missed their parents,
An incredible success time warrants,
Culprit time stolen years memories,
Claimed gold medal voyages stories, (5)

Settled abroad, he had a family nicely,
Affluent life learned renown precisely,
Sits often silently looks at his brother,
His photo frame picture is quite an allure, (6)

Knew his father and mother, teacher,
Life unrealistic impossibility, assure,
Assured, to reality, shelter felt divine,
Rolling tears in love, debtless refine, (7)

Unique brother's gift of courage owe,
Induced character pearl God, bestow,
Never seen God less questioned Him,
Why did he steal his parents, dream, (viii)

Took suddenly, one by one, surprised,
Manifested as his brother, life prized,
Love his elder brother more than soul,
Experienced his compassion to goal, (9)

He dreams for his tiny brother well,
Proved his sincerity, effort, time swell,
A thousand miles away, decades pass,
His settled life children, revive class, (10)

Have a loving parent, care infinite,
Compared to his brother, a rare insight,
Gratitude, fathomless and misnomer,
Blood links seemed eon soul enamor, (11)

A professor at a reputed university,
While coming back home in alacrity,
Got a long letter the native village sent,
His bedridden brother, kids absent, (12)

Without money, medicine, treatment,
Happened like a daydream nascent,
Villagers helped to the extent possible,
Still, his health deteriorates unable, (13)

The simple letter requested help sooner,
Choked his strength sat for an hour,
What happened, his brother failed,
Failed to intimate him a son wailed, (14)

Packed his belongings, resigned now,
Back to his native village prayer vow,
Serve Godly to save life determined,
The accord automatic blood defined. (15)

Acrimony

Inferno erupts in a calm ocean and stark,
The depth of the fathomless bottom is dark,
Refuses to dissipate burns fearsome,
The picture resembles the cursed hell known as,
Earth and breast tear up molten rock flow,
Devastation agitated lay insipid glow, (1)

Cursed a human heart acrimony hide,
Boiled as hell pit erupts venomous tide,
Fire burns fiery mind conscience blind,
Leads self-destruction life turbulent wind, (2)

Blind anger, uncontrolled chained the mind,
Enslaves and hearts cruelest, reason fails, find,
Anger controls the harsh tongue, a snake afire,
Words enact more than the sword, fearful dare,
Venomous fang strike never accept, timid,
Cursed acrimony hurt deadly act as rigid, (3)

Acrimonious state of mind far from reason,
Simmers within in guise torment all season,
Soul boils in anger, conscience fail to convince,
Wisdom misses guiding, consequences amiss,
Witness, ever a nation acrimony serpent swell,
People fueled in black rage catastrophe dwell,
Peace, discipline, amity, serving people in love,
Disappears quick, anarchy rule, amity dissolve,
Cursed acrimony motivated evil dwells,
Curses a time nation burns well, devils swell, (4)

Cursed humanity war never happens in a fight,
Lies mold acrimony caustic nation's eyesight,
War of words, threat, acrimony, ill comments,
At enmity, countries with deep hatred foment,
Humanity pays the cost bleeds innocent torment,
Curse acrimony weapon pretends innocent! (5)

Sweet home sapphire, blue diamond peace,
Family bond blood thicker, care n share bliss,
Mutual love accommodates rifts, delicate,
United mind n heart prevent irks and complicate,
Acrimony captures members, cursed ill fate,
Fractured diamonds to dust tongues irritate, (6)

Acrimony, willful arrogant, anger dowses quick,
Reject isolation of mind, evil lust hidden tragic,
Lust corrodes slowly; life loses thrust n energy,
Acrimony accumulated fuel devastating synergy,
Wise a person, rejects path, as host, acrimony,
Family home friend people smile in a symphony, (7)

Realizes a nation, peoples in between for peace,
Peace brings progress, future happiness, bliss,
Wiser a country, with people, shed acrimony total,
Amity in among nations acrimony turns mortal,
Acrimony is the stormy sea, lifeboat fears rock,
Conscience is a lighthouse that secures amok. (viii)

Admit To Life

Life infallible commit to blunder,
Rectify attitude get cautious after,
Alert mind, wise, detect error, clear,
Mistakes happen, but ignorant do endeavor,

Err is human nature often commit,
Guilt rectification intensely ways omit,
Accept committing an error, lesson win,
Righteous erroneous life harbor twin, (1)

Encompass yesteryears, darkness,
Committed mistakes in life often well,
Committed to hurting other hearts to swell,
Committed to when envy of others burns within,

Committed to arrogance yet ignored soul,
Committed to deprive rightful ignore all,
Committed to self joy forgot others soon,
Committed to earning wealth, never serving a lot,

Committed to self-service through others,
Committed to sin yet never felt, sadly bothers,
Committed for my life my world a motive,
Committed, for family, skip Lord active,

Committed to ignorance and purity erode fast,
Committed to rectifying blunder, try till last, (2)
Life incredible surprises shockwave jolt,
Outlook tumbles action amok yet revolt,

It came as a bolt shook frightened mind,
Never felt reason ever at sight a kind,
Sat silent, guilt sadden heart disturb,
The thinking was a weapon, led smart to throb,

Alone night long, fearful mind torment,
Sinful track selfish act rewind intent,
Console, shivering body affirms to resolve,
Thoughtful state time, confirms, absolves,

Better late than never, do listen to heart,
Listen to conscience ray glisten impact,
Focus on right and wrong in action choose,
Calm insight, right is an inclination to lose,

Turn to introvert life, brighter, more,
Inspire self-correction, thought pure,
Mind-sky inner, blue n bright, vision,
Found work n own path alight reason,

Felt innocent and ignorant in past condole,
Woke up to intuition guideline resolve,
Committed to tread in the path of truth n love, (3)
A small foot of man on the moon is significant,

A giant step of humanity means equivalent,
Admittance to infallible an acceptance firm,
Watershed of a transformed life, let reaffirm,
Better late than never essence of life target,
Purification of the heart absolves sin mitigate.
Past can't be rectified, sins can't be washable,
The best path right is to admit to life, infallible. (4)

AFFLICTION

The ego capture mind

Incredible ego is a tall mountain peak,
Enables ego to minimize low, a grass leaf,
Ego creeps into the mind a kid senses him,
Face, dress, names recognize self keen,

The ego is harmless, the essence of humanity grows,
Color, complexion, studies, health glow,
A ladder to raise, high in age, ego swells,
The mind gets a mate, cemented as oneself,

Conscience puzzles the mind or self to help,
Attributes of ego are chains in interlink,
The home of my parent cast status does wink,
Middle age accustomed humans to identity,
Name, education, clan, address visibility,
Career, occupation, degree reputation,
Sport, literature, art, music admirations,

At a crucial juncture, ego in life

Captured as a captive mind in chain tight,
Intoxicated mind in pride as kingmaker,
Life is from a blade of grass to a glass tower,
World notice in owing praises shower,

Speech visit help concern is top news,
Amazing a people listen to heart ruses,
Four walls of concrete a loner of the palace,
Friend, society, community traces,

Help, donate, and contribute to all shelters,
The heart is captive of its own fame and seeks a savior,
Freedom as a human lament private life,
Media is a hawk in the guise of a stalk with a knife,
A knife is lens world watch amused in time,
Expectation gets dry, hounding a pastime,

Conscience erases afflictions

Raise the curtain of mystic life curios,
Conscience prick leaves all spurious,
O soul, you are passing by track transient,
Never your credit, success but divine grace,

Your good deeds reaping dividend fine,
Once finished, you can find alone in time,
Friends people applaud fade in mist,
Media will conclude your memory in gist,

Sure, you shall depart the realm alone,
Your home, courtyard pet dog looks on,
Family kin will be at the front door in tears,
The Son of a friend will light a pyre and stand in prayer,

You came empty and will return like that,
Even your mortal remains in ash detach,
O soul, your face world only knows love,
Quit for good, face inclines to go above,

Only deeds will go with you like mate,
Good deeds give peace to bad ones torment,
Heartfelt the infinite pain agony cry out,
Ego replies caustic remark, mind in doubt,

Afflictions liberate freedom

Self accuses conscience of bitter imagination,
Point to conscience rude, indecent affliction,
Conscience gets hurt, telling fact, in the end,
O mind shed identify a sense of I point delusion,
I fuel ego, culprit-heart, is an affliction.
Conscience rescues the mind and listens to the wisdom
A captive of ego, break the chain to freedom

Afloat

A new millennium dawned in decades,
Human life is at the crossroad as it fades,
Smallpox, cancer, malaria, flue n rest,
In the past, human spirits tame n ruled best,

But changing times posed as unknown,
Science, research, to cure, exist none,
A virus, blowing the planet with infection, death,
First, it keeps spreading, blocking the breath,

Now antidote hopes to recover from Covid a bit,
It goes in weeks for life, hides asymptomatic,
A cataclysmic blow heart raises hope,
World at pray to Almighty, facing to solve,

May Lord save humans and plead only hope,
To walk the life till the rest safe to rope,
Deep hope is faith in time to face,
Deep hope is faith on You to guess,

Deep hope is in faith, in every breath,
Deep hope is in faith, in life differs from death,
Deep hope is a trace in the world of cures,
Deep hope humans Covid free sure,

Troubles neck deep but hope ablaze,
Self-sure in spirit, cross to work bravely,
The ultimate hope is feet firm n steady future,
Human intuition is guiding us forward to soar,

Through a whirlpool of events, a world in Lock,
Know a day shall come ashore from broke,
Economy, travel, work, education, health,
Peace n joy of life shines in length n breadth,

Some days may leave at age all normal,
On firm foot memories of birth-death dual,
On world works for serving all in spirit,
On hope descendants on earth grow bright,

To carry on our path of life counter again,
Bold ethics n faith guide do secure remain,
To serve n love humanity with no borders,
The human spirit is in joy, and freedoms keep order,

With continuity of life, hope aspiration rule,
Even time dreams and progress felt cool,
To walk the life till the rest, never one fear,
Love n hope for an eternity of life prevail, and sure,

New millennium God's grace, we hope future,
Though turbulent whirlpools of a river of lives,
The soul stays afloat in paradigm paralysis.

Air Of Menace

Know from teenage innocence gift,
Lifelong try to acquire failure drift,
Impossible, appear mind, evade nit,
Purity in life links, innocence greets, (1)

Alliance with truth integrity affirms,
Abhorrence for lies, guise, confirmation,
Detach the mind, abhorrent the thoughts,
Little souls lose peace and need effort, (2)

Like, simplicity, unassuming lead,
Admiration harbors in self indeed,
Rolls passionate, forward time wail,
Touching golden feather quite-fail, (3)

Cool, a mind contemplation lacuna hit,
Courage disappears, threats life wit,
World, paradise on earth fascinates me,
Unreal, spirit search in vain relate, (4)

Bed of roses path of life untrue bit,
Bed of thorn pierces limbs bleed nit,
Innocence, sacrificial goat, practice,
Save precious life shrewdness kiss, (5)

Truth, indeed I suffer, false for you,
Know, people never believe or view,
Fraught with danger, often irk fear,
Surrender instinct spit lies inferior, (6)

Unscrupulous mind exploitation all,
Plunder harsh world peace to recall,
Loot shelter food cloth means miss,
Innocence rest of life cry mirth wish, (7)

Forgo all freedom, equality, emotion,
Knows discrimination n indignation,
Torture breaks the spine, humiliates time,
Feel none act like savior secure fine, (viii)

Key-root critical for survival I discover,
The truth of my life, I gain violence, favor,
Cruelty radiate from, face demeanor,
Sock people dramatize my behavior, (9)

Blunt answer soaked with lies best,
Soft word falsehood pretense attest,
Crestfallen today, I admit guilt n sin,
Air-of-menace manage well, unseen, (10)

Survival of the fittest is a joke, the biggest,
Fang of snake hiss save life interest,
Never snake bite unless we provoke,
No need to touch its tail sleep evoke, (11)

Opens my heart, a true friend's week,
Avoid polite, humble, gentle dislike,
Not me n neighborhoods appreciate,
Obey, respond quickly, serve intricate, (12)

Threat on-air, pseudo postures arm,
Achieve everything in life with little harm,
Quit, air-of-menace, snake face death,
Kids play, hold snake tails lose breath, (13)

Alas

Watching searchingly, the scene,
A few men carrying the departed,
Bamboo poles, two parallel tied,
Tied with four bamboo sticks,

Threaded with cocoanut fiber tightly,
A few were followers shouting,
The name of Sri Ram is the only truth,
All other statements are utterly false,

Throwing puffed rice and coins,
Quiet speechless that struck me,
Is it Lord's name is truth and only truth?
Then why do people now remember,

Why do they recite when carrying the dead,
And rest of life ever remember Lord,
Every chanted His holy name?
Perhaps not, but a fact of our life,

This rice symbol food thrown,
Coins, a symbol of money, are thrown off,
Scattered on the road was the question,
And bluntly, vehemently, disturbingly,

Food and money are meaningless,
Only for the departed, not for the living,
So these items take place name of God,
Only bracket but within assets, accessories,

Thousands of them ever human dreams,
Utter these names silently till acquired,
Are they false? grumbles the mind,
Need this to survive desperately want them,

This dream I fumbled for a lifetime!
Surprisingly a lifetime these names took,
House, car, gadgets, furniture, ornaments,
The line is mile long but never tired,

When the departed one inert rested,
A few men carrying to the pyre chanting,
Once they are back home,
Immerse in worldly jobs,

And so quickly forgotten!
My children, my family, my life...
Endless this concept of mine,
I have built my home, got a family,

Achieved a promising career,
Confident, courageous, successful in life,
They devoted their entire time to this, worked hard,
Forgotten the only truth, Lord's name,

Objected vehemently, I have an idol of the Lord,
Worshipped Him, every day love Him,
Remember and pray when fallen sick,
My mind and its pretension,

If a human loves God in his lifetime,
Why this chanting to enlighten his spirit?
Alas, the treacherous mind,
Plundered a lifetime and its weapon, doubt,
I came home and knew,
The goal of life is to peruse the truth,
Alas, this illusion of glass and a gem.

Alert Invents

Dark a night front is opaque,
Abruptly halt forward compact,
Something happens within the shock,
Feet in motion stop as inert rock,

A gut feeling, the hair rises in fear,
Instinct warns the mind alert clearly,
A pit before, cliff at the edge, threat,
Alert a mind, totally blind create,

Create a focused survival instinct,
Backward safely covered distinct,
Life encounters threats to life rare,
Alert mind invents escape fare,

War is a test of valor threats most,
Moment poses do or die worst,
Alert mind provisions guise quick,
Escapes dangers in time explosive,

Alertness is the gift of destiny saves,
Sharpness lacks, kills blast waves,
Alert-mind courageous, hearts pour,
Forces defeat the attacking front core,

The alert mind of a leader turns quick,
Surprise invent, own enemy, a risk,
Win or defeat in merciless is a fight,
Alert invents surprise brave is sight,

Common is people are alert in public life,
Arsons, violence in the street, fast strike,
Innocent bleeds n lack a state alert,
Alert mind, life-saving tact, intimate,

Alert female save well stalker follows,
Alert, lacking insane killer face gallows,
Alert housewife, guess correctly market,
Alert family man, save income intricate,

Alert, adult conscious of future preplan,
Mind invents security n safe wiser is human,
Alert, senior, plan fitness of life, insure,
Alert is a keyword that solves, puzzles mature,

Narrate life experiences alert is inborn,
Wise or taught, practice, intense burn,
Who aspires there is a way, alert, invent,
Prosper in life, successful effort decent,

Alert in, game, alert to answer opponent,
Learned, cheats, magician alert efficient,
Alert rulers, army, and police defend well,
Alert a thief, mastermind, looter swell,

Alert crime, spies, intelligence serves,
Detective alert in hot pursuit deserves,
Concludes alert is a boon to a noble mind,
The boon to a goon devastates human life!

Excited alert kids win puzzles, crosswords,
Win games, result pink, adored forward,
Alert mind electric bulb, floodlight instant,
Daylight, opaque dark, hide, run, hesitant,

The kid shows ignorant key well unlocks,
Parent, teacher, public crazes alert kid rocks,
Alert is animal feature survival kit well,
Snake, mouse, tiger, deer, cat, dog smell,
Alert birds, plants, insects, and animal is a gift,
Gifted saves a life, haunts well, turns swift!

Alias In Veil

Long past in life, if probe ever,
Amazed as the face seen never,
Once the place it claimed of own,
Lo' to life the site is ever known,

The ground before Temple all around,
Never match a bit as sing-aloud,
The beachfront is there so is a temple,
But metamorphoses, if these got as simple,

The silence and solitude in the temple beauty on a beach,
Belies the enchanting stories as each,
The lane, the home in detail, disappeared,
I find these men home this time as cleared,

Nowhere were the men in the town, roads plain,
To search, find, talk a lot, in vain,
The school n College of memories lane,
But teachers and friends, it says never be the same,

Once visited my Alma Mater years back,
To find my root as this guy, alas, fear I lack,
This character in dreams sang about his own life,
Out of world fun pleasure study success bright,

Returned to my job, know not him ever,
It is absurd it looked like narrative dreams unreal n over,
Met in job number of people and home in detail,
But as if never remember anyone to prevail,

A family man once who built his home,
Had a wife decades ago, also had a son,
Feeling hopefully this man resembles my life,
As my wife, at a ripe age, says to her son with wife,

When I look at all these people at different times,
So different at a look, their world stories in lines,
Teenage youth adulthood family life n ripe age,
The wide gap in planes, their known outlook amaze,

One dies n fades in a swirl of time next gets born,
Reincarnation of spirit little symbol symptoms shown,
Each life with a dream attitude hobby in boots,
Habit thought love aspirations intense with root,

As check often first myself and each of them,
As if smiling at me much younger never be the same,
These days in silence, safe in age, feel so well,
Puzzled, amazed sojourn of soul alias in veil !!!

All Knowing

Every heart has an eye,
It can see pain n pleasure,
Sorrows behind smiles,
Tears behind the laughter,

Silence in front whispers,
Hope behind blankness,
Love behind care,
Serve behind compassion,

Truth in a veil of mute,
This eye fetches compassion,
With love n care,
Brings humanity into humans,

Brings nobility into insane,
Brings sweetness in dispassion,
Brings kindness to cruelty,
Brings angels in mortals,

Brings life to rot,
Brings dreams to drowsiness,

Brings rainbows in dark clouds,
Brings a spectrum of colors in the prism of look,

Tears perish to wrinkles in smiles,
Mirage of oasis perishes dreary quicksand,
Crimson dawn, melts hunting night,
Rose perishes fear of pricking thorns,

Ignorance vanishes to the Light of knowledge,
Drisha, your painting,
Speaks expressive mind,
Speaks on butterflies in the moonlit sky,

Speaks on pearls strewn conspicuous,
On the golden sand beach of the blue sea,
Not art but awareness,
Not stardust but silvery moonlight,

Not a dew of blade of grass,
But dew a streak of lights in the dawn,
Very rare, but with the grace of the divine,
May Lord Grace you on microscopic vision.

In the eye of your passionate heart,
Love you dear, well,
I perceived from thousand miles away,
Away, amazed and speechless….
Messages of the new generation,
Crystals shine continental apart.

Allures Alluvial Soil

Thrilling youths accept challenges, all,
Struggle-hard study difficult embroil,
Burn midnight lamp, success sincere,
Determinations, focus mingles sheer, (1)

Destination foreign shores education,
Dreams lifelong, passionate devotion,
The day of reckoning n brings good news,
Secures success reward degree muse, (2)

Extraordinary performances acclaim,
Offshore invitations reach live inflame,
Immense desires dream manifest best,
Degree highest award recognition test, (3)

Bon voyage arrival sudden life change,
The university, new environment edge,
New life initiates study friendship like,
Teacher library hostel metropolis hike, (4)

Language lifestyle is marvelous intimate,
Food, dress, demeanor, talk intoxicate,
Hardship bear fruit reward fetches job,
Standard life apartments heartthrob, (5)

Revelation enamor succulent comfort,
Innovative minds attract applause but,
Affluence luxurious lifestyles and family,
Never heard, imagined, discovered truly, (6)

Decade rolls ambitions fulfilled entice,
Entices not present yesteryears, notice
Often heart searches, solace, silence neat,
Solitudes life recluse to nature retreat, (7)

The soil, verdure forest hill, meadows,
Merges soul, complete golden windows,
Wet earth scent fume rain drop cause,
Aromas spread sensuous limbs pause, (viii)

Season change blossoms colorful best,
Fragrance pervades, steals heart interest,
Enchants river winds morn dusk neat,
Heart allures alluvial soil find discreet, (9)

Flood tears disobey surprises, are sudden,
Why! Native soil gravitate eye moisten
Sacred land incites reminiscence scratch,
Motherland, most beautiful love match, (10)

Childhood, a fertile soil lives nourished,
Golden cornfield inhale air flourished,
The dustbowl evening cloud cow herd,
Bells on neck ring fairylands absurd, (11)

Unambiguous village kids play amaze,
Distant memories entangle lives craze,
Sits alone amidst velvet grass field nit,
Recline sprawl limbs look skies intuit, (12)

Nights star-studded dark skies the same,
Allure alluvial soil, childhood inflame,
Silent Night n skies whisper is universal,
Rebels heart to journey home enthrall, (13)

Intoxicate life impossible time embroil,
Lament soul home allures alluvial soil.
Calls homeland intense feeling capture,
Worlds apart, I discover a stark future. (14)

Amalgam

Intensify storm dark cloud cover,
Lightening n thunder, I shudder,
Thoughts frighten, the storm within,
Steal loud cries sight replica dim, (1)

Ocean of tear flood neighborhood,
Poverty sickness amalgam, brood,
Merciless time death vulture love,
Heartbroken peace smile dissolves, (2)

Snatch precious life void of distress,
Vagary of melancholy time's mess,
Lonely city mall school college nit,
Broken homes, miserable dispirit, (3)

A city of sorrows overwhelms pain,
Bustling road milling crowd wane,
Somber looks people sad, confined
Ambient amalgam and solitudes define, (4)

Wildlife forest reserve the picture,
Tourist spots empty lodge harbor,
Waterfall, mountain place vacant,
Treasure trove lakes wait, vibrant, (5)

Coastal beach havens have few tourists,
Speculates mind disappear trysts,
Years roll demise flatter to depict,
Tourist heavens desolate, deplete, (6)

Endless my thought squalls here,
Landscape sketches despair clear,
Anticipate thunderstorms, a sock,
Destroy homes city in the dark, amok, (7)

Ambient amalgam states my mind,
Inner life stormy night fears wind,
Wind of perilous predicament writ,
Clueless, see bright future I greet, (viii)

Swollen hopeless nightmares melt,
Health n happiness people to a belt,
A new dawn brings messages to heal,
Salvage spirit afresh images, reveal, (9)

Lifts lockdown travel ban, all total,
Globetrotting begins n book portal,
Noisy, busy city life, nit once again,
Mean to survive work class regain, (10)

Smiles, my people, their hearty faces lit,
Scars heal sooner than I lose wit,
Forgets agonies departed dear soul,
Wipe tear quick, I mingle, soon goal, (11)

My land regains heaven n paradise,
Love induces heart I never ostracize,
Wait impatient, cherish prosperity,
Embrace brotherhood in impunity, (12)

Good news, goodwill, I feel fragrant,
Dark thoughts once I tremble rant,
Forsake inhibition, resurrect spirit,
Watch bright sunshine mirth greet, (14)

School bus passes, kid crowd, laugh,
Sketch resurgent mine spiral graph,
Wish dreamy-night, pleasure, balm,
No qualms, I ink ambient amalgam. (15)

Ambiguity

Amazes mind puzzle complexity,
Human all strand, really duplicity,
Search in vain true self in guise,
Ornate titles misguide exercise, (1)

Claim public servant yet master,
Exhibit humility n control power,
Watch kind-hearted people, love,
Distribute food cloth peace dove, (2)

Seek news from the admired public,
Police discover a hoarder n tragic,
Scarce commodity stores n wait,
Hike prices artificial profit great, (3)

Behaves like learning to teach kids,
A long session on morality reads,
Teach well on subjects all advice,
Demand to enroll in tuition suffice, (4)

Teach money corrupts lo, collect,
Coaching center, money, spin bet,
Enough character, build process,
Love people talk friendly impress, (5)

Clean life, hands clean, no corruption,
Pure heart, trusts simple options,
Mind is pure and rejects discrimination,
Reject hatred of class caste none, (6)

Reject anger, little violence n harm,
Reject greed, value, integrity warm,
Practice care for follows needy souls,
Share sympathy help empathy all, (7)

Teach parents earnest, ever belief,
Deal face trouble n honesty relief,
Muse kids grow adults follow a scent,
Know parents talk all act different, (viii)

My highest technical self is an engineer,
Doctor, lawyer, scientist, life secure,
Incredible society bribes corrupt,
Enlighten yet honey-trapped rust, (9)

Craze money sweeter than honey,
Shed ethics embrace rich's cronies,
Hike personal fees cross all logic,
Beyond reaches of poor, sock magic, (10)

Democracy plays clarion equality,
Rule constitution same oath duty,
Leaders held a ceremony solemn nit,
Betrayal to people real, drama lit, (11)

Lit, news, tributes, benevolent life,
Deny ticket for election gets strife,
Oath serves nations, people devout,
Consolidate family with clan clout, (12)

Punish opponents deprive benefit,
How much hypocrisy, class inflict,
Endless suffering and agony soak all,
Endemic diseases n gold enthrall, (13)

The law can't reinforce reform people,
Truly knowledge adherence is simple,
Practice, integrity, clean life, divine,
Ameliorate ambiguity lands shine, (14)

Looking at myself in a mirror if duplicate,
Part of people, period true indicates,
Truth bites every human feels pain,
Equally, guilt hurt me inks inflame. (15)

AMBIT

Abominable life obnoxious duty,
Caretaker of a house tag beauty,
Impressionable outer sight glow,
Name the famous mansion to owe, (1)

The name is PROMISE hallowed lit,
Bright color floral bedecked hit,
Living here for decades to maintain,
Life single loneliness in disdain, (2)

The community bears the cost well,
PROMISE lived the family swell,
Four generations, a century-long,
Most renowned a family life in song, (3)

Influential people rich in business,
They spread worldwide impress,
Affluent, educated, artist, thinker,
Family grasped knowledge more, (4)

Respected the community liked,
Immense contribution life hiked,
A significant house of the town link,
In a few years, fight families sink, (5)

Bitter quarrel irrupted over right,
Right turned misnomer tore tight,
A gruesome sight, violent revenge,
Parents, siblings, direct avenges, (6)

Same blood united for a century,
PROMISE sheltered life mercury,
Mercurial the love, care, affection,
Dreaming prosperity commotion, (7)

Overflow unity, I served faithfully,
Illiterate knew poison doubtfully,
Suspicion crept stealthily, strong,
Advice interpreted claim wrong, (viii)

Accused each other, and inimical,
Trust fades quickly, talk minimal,
Death prowled rooms, suspicious,
One by one, all left, reign furious, (9)

Link disconnected cutoff relation,
Fled far-flung cities dent emotion,
The mere caretaker was a servant here,
Knew each family member, fear, (10)

Any of them little visited, inspect,
Once tagged PROMISE introspect,
Promised, lived united gold venom,
Doubted the action raze suspicion, (11)

Jealousy, cold anger fueled by visible,
Heard the angry voice of life crumble,
The last person in the family gave the keys,
Staying here for years alone but ease, (12)

Look at PROMISE beautiful sight,
Flowers blossom in spring excite,
Feel tearful brokenhearted write,
To the great grandfather his right, (13)

Still living abroad but request,
He once rebuilt the house to his best,
Squandered his wealth lovingly,
PROMISE stood attractive incredibly, (14)

Getting unwell faithful lifelong,
To hand over the keys it belongs,
Ambit to perform as caretaker,
No way possible life is premature. (15)

Ambivalence

Inexhaustible energy fountain,
Green forest rapids, mountains,
Treasure troves hideous invite,
Tired bones, fatigue mind excite, (1)

Nature's gift human greed class,
Ambivalence looks through glass,
Human recluse n sheds tension,
Resurrect from ruins if mentioned, (2)

Fresh air, clean water, intimate,
Romantic mood dusks dictate,
Effusion of sensations counter,
Devastation project an answer, (4)

Morning mist lose myself lame,
Sunshine in brilliance to tame,
Lovelorn walk abandon I move,
Charred trees fire smoke wove, (5)

Rain in forest rivulets enamor,
Waterfall river swell wind lure,
Tore wounds in my heart heal,
Barren field dirt, mud me kills, (6)

Flees life to summer resort cool,
Cold wind, cool a shade wonderful,
Greenery fresh afternoon excite,
The lake vanishing sadden light, (7)

Boathouse hideout life unwinds,
Misery, sorrow, agony, erase kind,
Pelican flamingos migrate delight,
Seasons arrive, late I miss a sight, (Viii)

Spring brings intense pleasure,
Pink, crimson, yellow, blue color,
Red, white flower fragrant steal,
Misses a heart, late a fall reveal kill (9)

Ink canvas of my pattern of life,
Wish nature I recover from faces strife,
Spreads epidemic lessons worth,
Vanishes verdure, barren earth, (11)

Listen to the waves crash loud,
Blue ocean watches a silent cloud,
Cloud mind bottom ambivalent,
Plastic poison lacks benevolence (12)

Time disappoints, discovers a cocoon,
Sleep long, wait, nature cure soon,
Metamorphose my life into a butterfly,
The pain of caterpillar memory, a lie, (13)

Moonlit night jasmine blossom,
Butterfly me amuses awesome,
My nature is ephemeral pretense,
Nature best grows, in ambivalence, (14)

Ameliorated

Alarmed peace joy eloped socking,
Remembers birth of first child jubilations,
Apple eye of parent pampered loved,
Intense care, a playful only son, worth,

Fruit of endless prayers, God graced,
His family overwhelmed him growing nicely,
School going, good at study, disciplines,
Satisfied teachers, got appreciation a lot,

Awards in competition, cups in sports,
The glowing high-school result applauded,
Mother was so happy, Father was content,
Beautiful home happiness stayed,

Homely feast, festival, journey arrives and go,
Son getting youth college life passing,
Father discovers son smoking in streets,
Among guys cheering strangers, comment,

Clean dressed got dirty, shabby treatment,
Disrespect, increasing to elders, curses,
Demanding money, scooter, mobile,
Unnoticed visits to nearby cities with friends,

Coming late at night, no answer for his dad,
A wall of mistrust and anger captured my heart,
Captured the heart of the father, modest income,
Shattered with the behavior of a child, his future,

Heartbroken, the poor man losing balance,
Irritated scolds the mom of the child harshly,
Silent by now, Mother lost faith in life, cries,
Weeps inadvertently before neighbors,

Little speaks to others, her world crumbling,
Getting sick, pale, scanty food, sits mute,
Wait patiently for her son for lunch, dinner,
Absence pushing mother leaving food,

Never asking son the reason or studies,
Rowdiness explicit, with a long hair beard,
Mustaches, open shirt, dirty shoes,
Comes home drunk, these days, very late,

Dropped the college, now jobless, a waste,
No more home feasts inviting relatives, neighbors,
A sweet home, now dark, gloomy, silent,
Discussed neighbors, relatives, and elders condemn,

The child is beyond correction, hardly listening,
Demands parents, the threat often nerve-shattering,
Fragile female bones couldn't bear the torture,
Shattered, facing sickness lays on a bed,

Father cooks food, feeds medicine, a stone,
Never both talk with the son rarely eats,
Complaints growing in the community angry,
The mother fell unconscious, driven to a hospital,

Lack of blood, urgently required by the doctor,
The husband's blood didn't match,
Not available in a blood bank, father called son,
Dashed to the hospital, found her mom dying,

Checked his blood matched,
He was sharing his blood while sleeping in bed,
Adjacent, he looked at Mom, and her sense returned,
She told feebly, let me die, hating her life,

Folded her hands, she was pleading, sobbing,
Son sat near her, looked sober if understood,
His mom returned home after a weak,
The child was a changed person, silent,

Exhibited obedience, behaved gently, left friends,
Joined college after years of studying,
Got the highest percentage graduated one day.
Applied for a fine job today successfully,

With the call letter son was telling his mom,
I am going out ma, joining for a job,
Mother was thinking about how he ameliorated!
Kissed his forehead, blessed, Dad, watching.

Anchor

Anchor of my life, superior,
Mental support and savior,
Wedlock surprises n unites,
Man-wife walk duet recite, (1)

Face unknown trust, know,
Home boat sail lovers glow,
Weathers turbulence excels,
An anchor to the opposite well, (2)

Wife weeps on shoulder nit,
Raise strength of mind, wit,
Trouble, pain, fever do visit,
Serve I console empathy lit, (3)

Harsh world, a battle I face,
Failure error humiliates Lace,
Disappoint actions, fruitless,
Futile attempt soul depress, (4)

Soul mate usher confidence,
Present her anchors intense,
All dedication and sympathy mixed,
Calm advice, intimate love, fix, (5)

Family life is fabulous, sustaining,
Frivolous mind hazard tame,
Anchor wildlife cover nature,
Incredible protection secure, (6)

Shelter safe weather climate,
Wildlife roam-free n primates,
Meadows n forest surround,
Brook ravines water sounds, (7)

Hides offspring nature's care,
Cliff, crevasse cave soil share,
Mountain and river gorges project,
Highland marshy field detect, (viii)

Animal, bird, fish, creature nit,
Breed nicely, feed discreetly,
Mother Nature balances life,
Immaculate n helps in strife, (9)

Nourish nature raises anchor,
Ambience-of-anchor hanker,
Anchor human life on Earth,
Ever serve, care, love, n worth, (10)

Continent ocean sky n wind,
Seasons in queue help kind,
The fertile Earth, bountiful grain,
Mighty River crisscross train, (11)

Train human spirit endeavor,
Food water village city more,
People find the Earth unique,
Mother Earth tolerates, piques, (12)

Humans exploit ruthless land,
Forest water air pollutes hand,
Amaze the Earth protects life,
Resurrect human limit strife, (13)

Rebuild nature, automatic nit,
Realizes human life, live or quit,
Ambiance-of-anchor persists,
Fresh wind, water, rain insists, (14)

Heals bitterness soul cherish,
Prosper amity peace flourish,
The earth ambiance of the anchor,
Tell humans in peril, life to secure. (15)

Anchorage

Tumults of thought memory storm,
Departures teenage reminder learn,
Grow my existence under-shadow,
Limitless love care project window, (1)

Immaculate attention protects most,
Ignorance, wild mind waylaid, trust,
Trusts, watchful eyes advise respect,
Innumerable troubles save dissect, (2)

Umbrellas safeguard perilous, time,
Grievous mistake commit I incline,
Wayward mind slips feverish swim,
Recall the blue water of the river warn win, (3)

Depth of river unknown whirlpool,
Undercurrent calm, stern look, cool,
Prowling nighttime unsocial harm,
Dusk initiates, lantern-lit study arm, (4)

Conscious of his presence, discipline,
Habit increases concentration clean,
Marvel student life exam result nit,
Excel career higher anchorage writ, (5)

Overwhelm influence nurture soul,
Sizzle paternal characters seize goal,
Simple life, reject opulence, humble,
Truthful, silent, demeanor life gentle, (6)

Hardworking, kind, considerate soft,
Inherit all qualities conscience loft,
Innumerable hardships practice all,
Encounter troubles often yet enroll, (7)

Mental support brief guidance well,
Paternal love care goodwill to swell,
Face harsh world mutinous life rise,
Witness brute mind, savage precise, (viii)

Forgets noble heart indwells nature,
Anger, greed, jealousy, cruelty, favor,
Revolt self paternal guides interfere,
Invisible chain lifelong feel superior, (9)

Quell mutiny, repent, feel guilty soul,
Citadel of fame, a name that realizes a goal,
Cement effort father's stubborn role,
Deny forthright any credit pats troll, (10)

Education higher affluence his gifts,
Obedience accrued my love, nil rifts,
Strongest bond invisible, lot cherish,
Giant tree father upon head nourish, (11)

Cool shades of foliage, paternal grace,
Little exhibits his pride smile interlace,
Inner heart see temple his abode tall,
Father no more in mortal world recall, (12)

The eldest son did light his pyre, cremation,
Solemn pledges to adhere to his ethics won,
Surrender my ego at his feet, do pray,
Temptation in life, corrode little betray, (13)

Never betrayed my father's faith, my grit,
My obeisance till death worship strict,
Dedicate my poem of love realization,
Cherish the memory of his contribution, (14)

His presence lives in my heart, prefer,
Reminiscences father's voice enamor.
Anchorage chains tight storm endure,
Awestruck anchorage lights his picture. (15)

ANGUISH

Recalls, nature, and elegant moods,
Attracts heart, magnetic woods,
Hypnotizes tranquil forest well,
Peace, happiness, fantasy swell, (1)

Sooth gentle breeze passion nit,
Forgets life troubles pleasure lit,
Aberration of a spectral light nail,
Catches sight of a heavenly trail, (2)

Silence penetrates the mind, a song,
Giant tree wild-flowers live long,
Distant mountain mystery test,
Riverine meadows I recline rest, (3)

Ornate bridal dress, why discard,
Furious mood nature ruin hard,
Storm sweep with horror and dismay,
Anguish aberrations n fears stay, (4)

Shifts my focus, mesmerizes my soul,
Paradise on earth loves goals,
Remind realm name, aspiration,
A face world recognizes the motion, (5)

Charisma cherishes joy in opulence,
Dream hope intimate confluence,
Enchanting beauty, her spell test,
Young minds seek her touch rest, (6)

Charming children smile, laugh,
Focus my life on the pleasure graph,
Perplex, life raises a melodrama,
Breaks spine of strength enigma, (7)

Accident, illness, death, departure,
Humiliation sufferance al' torture,
Forces spirit amid solitude weep,
Anguish aberrations rare n reap, (viii)

Aberration self-chosen surprises,
Anguish in vain lesson surmises,
Retracts focus from pensive sight,
A treasure trove within nit delight,
Close eyes search my heart allure,
Love is pure nectar, kindness yore, (9)

Compassion golden bricks in a lock,
Devotion surrenders humility rock,
Courage, trust, and noble nature sprout,
King of golden lands mind n shout, (10)

Desire replicates in mirrors ponder,
Endless hungry mind loot, plunder,
Ecstatic mood spirit now lost total,
Forgets quick poor life limb mortal, (11)

Helluva hell capture a mind within,
Lust loses control n disasters ruin,
Worry, tension, fear, anger, ego grips,
Elusive is mind, wishes to conquer trips, (12)

Sorrows cast dark valley pain hunt,
Kingdoms within visit horror taunt,
Laughter smile terrifies the mind shudder,
Anguish aberrations n I miss rudder, (13)

Ink saga of contemplations intense,
Pure, pristine nature n Realm sense,
The purity of the soul is fragrant innocence,
Divine own nature aberration sentence,
Anguish aberrations n ruin pretense,
Burn forest of thoughts ash remains. (14)

Animate

Socking the gruesome sight crowded,
Billowing dark fumes, tongues of fire,
Burning the high-rise building houses,
Loud cries of people at height waving,

The specter pleading for help saving a life,
Who are you uniformed men daring,
Fighting sparing own life rises on a ladder,
Pour water jet through windows, balconies,

Enters into smoking windows daredevil,
High apartment lives choked unconscious,
No way to come down life closed,
Staircases engulfed by fire confined,

Clueless trying to jump to death,
The wrong choice to save life fail decision,
Just this moments enter these men,
Lifts limbs drained out of energy,

Through rope ladder platform rescue,
Hours of these horrible scene fight,
Continues till the deathly inferno off,
Extinguished the fire, charred lives,

Devastated families, horrible death occur,
A life that matters a few seconds save,
The blackened faces burning eyes search,
Recover senseless, dying children, babies,

Spine chilling actions wordless achieve,
The saga of firefighters amid ruins,
Crawl among amber, intense heat,
The action final, end operations, back,

A big megapolis explosions miles away,
Fire and black smoke touches the sky,
Destroyed adjacent buildings, traffic,
Cordon off the entire crowd, danger zone,

Bystander observes people agitated,
Burning people within the fuel station,
Shouting excited pushing the rope,
Blocked by these death-defying men,

Cool, and calm, highly trained,
Managing irate crowd make way,
Let the vehicles firefighter move in,
Fire extinguishers spray chemicals,

A more dangerous place may explode,
Trembles me they walk through smolder,
Fight the operation nerve-wracking,
The toxic fume, heat, live working,

A few days the hell fire put-off now,
Leaves devastation, destruction,
A few lives were lost, wounded rescued,
Savior of human life unlisted,

News, how many survived, property saved,
These brave men disappear like a ghost,
Look at them have worried families,
Purposefully children kept out of father,

It happens such savior succumbs,
Wait, family desperate heard the news,
Sacrificed the life, not at war field,
But saving own people in dire threat,

No way means the job, skill, and courage,
Tearful inks saluting immortal spirits,
Walking on a road footpath traffic jam,
Listen to blaring sirens speeding cars,

Divided the road to the side, opens fast,
Blocked green signals to halt let fire-men,
The men in helmet stand ringing the bell,
The eyes of people viewing them,

Standstill on a footpath, drivers notice,
I found these faces animate unique,
Rarely I saw these hopeful eyes sparkle,
Praying for their spirit salute bravery,
Animate the air fast and quick happen,
Lingers deep gratitude a fire has shaken

ANTIQUE

Golden age, untraceable detail,
Sparkle antique stones unravel,
Thousands of years, a cruel time,
Erased legacy of brightest mind,

Incredible imaginative fascination,
Executive artwork in rock glistens,
Antique city ancient ruins remake,
The bank of the sea mimics surging waves,

Devastated, in an invasion, traces were lost,
Sand dunes immortal taunts most,
Coastal storms, winds, salty mingle,
Priceless antiques are amiss as brittle,

Pristine, a river dissecting the city,
Indistinct sand bed, dirt drain pity,
Stone-wall embanks round ponds,
Freshwater is clean for a sacred bond,

Antique prehistoric saline underneath,
Wonderful ponds a hundred feet beneath,
Narrow lanes, brick houses, close,
A dozen feet higher than roads owes,

Lanes, narrow, century-old, brick paths fine,
Time changed as concrete serpentine,
Antique kerosene lamp posts vanish,
Time swept the development electric kiss,

Ancient temples, antique idols sizzle,
Ancient faith allure pilgrims to mingle,
Morning n evening crowd prayer,
Bare feet dancing, ecstatically admire,

Festivals' antique traditions exist,
Generations converge trust, persist,
Ancient-warrior fights enacted a year,
The procession moves slowly in lanes clear,

Sword, costumes, drums, firecrackers,
Reminds a race of brave, mighty fighters,
Symbol of antique kingdom reminisce,
Bank of the Ganga to the Godavari remains,

Celebration of Dussehra idols earthen,
Divine mother decorated antique tradition,
For a couple of weeks, ancient worship recreates,
Immersion in the river, holy moth initiates,

Sacred the beach, ponds, antique faith,
Early morning bath, temple visit wealth,
Detached from family life, widows in vows,
An ancient practice in the city, austerity glows,

Vegetarian month, purity in practice,
Concludes with boating in the morning,
Bright race voyages symbolize missing,
Neither the valor nor voyages in a stormy sea,

Nor executives rock carvings king's glee,
Antiques exist in festivals in celebration,
Car festival in city catches admiration,
Deities in a chariot pulled with rope in the crowd,
Antique ancient faith absolves a mix of pride.

Apostle Of Peace

Jesus

When human-mind raises a war,
Love, brotherhood, mercy debar,
Anger, ego, greed, and cruelty declare,
Lusts for wealth n building an empire,
Wonderful city in razing n despair,
Civilization at zenith sinks total,
Amazing miracle, it forgets mortals,
Eon human mind search eternity,
Amidst ruins time query stupidity,
Supremacy rules race, color, skin,
Love discrimination brutal means,
Apocalyptic horror draws canvas,
Heal an apostle of peace shields morass,
Preach love and care for precious life,
Hands mean to serve to reject knives,
Merciful mind, heart with compassion,
The selfless dedication to life passion,
Usher human hope help confides,
Gentle touch erases evil, love rides, (1)

Buddha

Ancient past, kingdoms in an invasion,
Famine, hunger, and slavery a common,
Civilization in ruins cities, obliterated,
The apostle of peace rose to promulgate,
Taught detachment n non-violence,
Preached truth, compassion, intense,
Kingdoms in oppression got peace,
Lord Buddha brought peace n bliss,
Kalinga war littered a lot of corpses,
River red in blood, afloat dead horses,
Atop Dhauli hill, King Asoka witnesses,
Buddhist monk console king depressed,
King Asoka renounced all conquest,
Apostle of peace indoctrinated best, (2)

Gandhi

The nation was in utter darkness and peril,
Colonial rulers were cruel, plundered at will,
Famine, hunger, and sickness visit often,
Fear, pain, torture, future uncertain,
People in slavery were unhappy tense,
Freedom of opinion complains offense,
Peace, love, friendship, kindness lost,
Caste, creed, race, language wall most,
Subjugated to alien rule n spineless,
Apostles of peace appeared and impressed,
Avatar of non-violence, truth protest,

Demanded freedom of nation severest,
Peaceful protest, fasting, mass rejection,
Apostle of peace peacefully brought freedom,
Centuries of darkness melt happier,
The country is peaceful and never secure, (3)

Red Cross

Humans saw the birth of the Red Cross in war,
Selfless volunteer treat wounded care,
Where humanity is lost n death play,
Human kills or cripple human, in gay,
Mercy, compassion, and love are forgotten,
Violent battles erase life heart bottom,
Red Cross brings life to a dying wish,
Proclaims Red Cross apostle of peace (4)

Apotropaic Amulet

Teenage life fascinates most,
Adventure thrills dearly cost,
Scolds parent warn frequently,
Saves an Apotropaic amulet, (1)

Innocence trust time assure,
Wonder in forest little to fear,
Queer voice noise jolts group,
Run, apotropaic prayer coup, (2)

Believe amulets protect often,
Dilapidated houses in caution,
Nighttime shadows terrify me a lot,
An Amulet prevents ghosts and boasts, (3)

Midnight story of demon witch,
Dream adds further n beseech,
Grandparent rebukes, narrate,
Keep in hand tight an amulet, (4)

Why do you laugh, and I only trust,
In youth n adulthood, at almost,
Humiliation, threat, when tested,
Feel amulet presence is best, (5)

Worship n apotropaic nature,
Fever in trouble agrees secure,
Agree you say my blind belief,
Cold fear all time brings relief, (6)

Incredible human nature host,
Dark mind raise surreal most,
Blind belief true or false enact,
Courage, a calm mind will react (7)

A modern century man contest,
Old fashion blind notions reject,
My mother, old age evening wait,
Wicker in the lamp-lit pray late, (Viii)

Exist well an apotropaic amulet,
Marriage travel is distant intimate,
Ah.. people do divorce, accidents,
Ruin life sure if amulet prevent, (9)

Black magic, the dark world survives,
Erases faith clean, yet it revives,
Apprehension fear to dominate,
Traditions and customs promulgate (10)

My child laughs at amulet best,
We keep smile check exam next,
Son's amulet and daughter's locket,
Examination time keep top-secret, (11)

Kids watch the ship to inaugurate,
A cocoanut is broken elaborately,
At least you talk, my friend nut,
Apotropaic amulet locket a trust, (12)

Trusts we forfeit, conscience rot,
Never oppose ego greed not,
Surrender to bitter fights, quarrel,
Legacies exist n good omen, revel, (13)

Appall Your Lies

Life is pure

Contemplate human nature,
Born like crystal glints pure,
Humans part of earth beings,
Naked animal fish bird sings,
Blue sky, ocean, lake, or river,
Green forest meadows allure,
Nature without a veil, project,
Pretense deceptions do reject,
Reject guise impurity or lies,
Human, nature pure precise, (1)

Lies disguise

Ship iron built crosses, oceans,
Prevents water inside the reason,
Start iron corrodes, ships sink
Human-mind pollute life blink,
Intelligence, memory, thought,
Mind manipulate all, wrought,
O' Lion's heart, cover body vanity?

Mind deceives first, eons dignity,
A dress, costume, ornaments,
Mind disguise beautifully vents,
Softens talk, smile, loving eyes,
Anger within, appall your lies, (2)

Pretentious lies

The look demeanor suave lure,
All that glitter isn't gold and pure,
Love friendliness, sharing heart,
Often soaked with motive a fact,
Selfless portrayal cons a selfish,
Exploitation deception nets fish,
Mind got blind to seek greed, lust,
Jealousy, anger, cruelty, almost,
Your nature corrodes life sinks,
Perplex, mind betrays, yet winks
Troubles of life sink placid moan,
Inner pain, hurt, fear, tension,
Anxiety, misery, clueless, worries,
Still pretends n appall your lies, (3)

Lies of culprit mind

Proclaim you love your world,
The world is family friend gold,
Ever include parent, kid, blood,
Express their love, warmth, bold,
What lips utter sweet feels cold,

Tip of iceberg n harmless mold,
Heart concedes flatters, praise,
Batter deals of, give n take, haze,
O' Lion's heart, inhuman deal,
The parent left, family and friends feel,
I, me, mine means a real to throb,
Heart conceals total, nature rub,
Human nature is pure n precise,
Culprit mind act, appall your lies, (4)

Lies fade before righteous

Control mind, tie with heart well,
Hearts, driven by conscience, swell,
Conscience derails, temptation fuels,
Lifestyle, righteous, lifetime effort tell,
Train alert disciplines, mind to size,
Lion's heart, no more appall your lies (5)

Applause

Clap to whom?
To only you, your ego,
Your illusion, delusion,
Console my image in the mirror,

Simple life solitude savor,
Saw huge roaring applaud,
Great acts in folded hands,
Smiles, powerful bends, bold,

Puzzles mass get blind sold!
In the silence continue my whispers,
Keep your distance from the spoiling mess,
Born wise, one steals success,

Born and dumb, blind, inert mind
Divine play, human unkind,
Applause in crescendo vibrates
Only who befriend victory

At easy, ruthless n quick,
Destiny grace a few rest not,
Hunger money desire trot,
The world is a stage fighting in a fix,

Intellect reflex practice mix,
The game is fun most, applaud,
The winner fetches applause,
Education career community

All are fields in a fight so tight,
Wit and deception con conquer,
Rags to riches capture power,
Loot open alibi service care,

Poor destitute applaud loudly,
Dark ladder to the top of the cloud,
Incredible reel life in the realm,
Humanity sings success aplomb,

Applause is the only food for the soul,
Creator surprises, is it your goal?
Humanity is never a failure in total,
Few but serve suffering immortal,

Applause never seek to lie low,
Later, the community honors n bows,
No one applauds but sings in love,
Keep the divine spirit above,

Applaud in mass a roar,
Artists, singers, actors, savor,
A creative mind gets inspired,
Applause is roses and admiration,

Rarest gems in human fascination,
Address in the mirror to myself,
Eyes must go inward, face,
Outer world illusive entraps,

Inner focus truth encompasses,
Applauses intoxicate the mind,
Addiction to ego peace perishes,
Hunger for praise is a fire,

Wisdom burns rules desire,
Your life is mysterious,
A helping hand serving people,
And needy are watched,

Up by creator, amazed,
If He has a heart, it melts,
In love n divine love
Guides one to the path of light,

Darkness, then one sees,
Whom one helped once,
No one else than He,
Life changed for eternity,

One sees everyone,
As the embodiment of the divine,
And play here in life serene.
Peace, bliss, and happiness pours in,

The grace of the divine is if only yours.

Apprehension

Intuitive natural wonder

Blue planet invest in unique nature,
Blue skies, blue ocean n verdure,
Brown earth white beach entices,
The greenery of a forest, floral impress,
Icy peak snow-white fears molten,
Dawns at icy slopes excite, golden,
Sunrise sunset crimson lot spray,
Bountiful golden crop wind sway,
Lake, pond acquire stars n moon,
Placid river glisten sunlight soon,
Bridal dress charming lady cites,
Perplex life apprehension intuits, (1)

Amazingly rain arrives

Earth being thrills path of roses,
Born n walk, depict poesy poses,
Bridal dress fades out n thunder,
Lightning strike blitz if shudder,
Flood flurry sudden cyclone, twit,

Peace, tranquility erase loses wit,
Scintillating beauty smacks quit,
Life alerts, apprehension intuits, (2)

Scintillating urban life

Happy people, merrymaker loft,
Peaceful landscape lovely most,
Life progresses well mirth shower,
Busy life pattern wealth power,
Power of pink health, joy travel,
Wonderful time human unravel,
Night finds awake, dance parlor,
Game, festive season mind savor,
Dawn break, good news forecast,
A dark cloud hangs tense overcast,
Pandemic viral, people if clueless,
Infects, system collapse, distress,
Wildcat nation strike violent hot,
Arson, fire, destruct angers most,
Life n death deal protest recruits,
People hope apprehension intuits, (3)

Shields balanced mind

Daydreamer shrugs from a window,
Apprehension, intuition gut show,
More thought clouds mind terrify,
Live in present calm future notify,
Intellect wise memory experience,

Find survival path solve, immense,
Close eyes ears tight lips pretense,
Life safe focus, thoughtless hence,
Attitude nature feeling sensations,
Positive n negative call indications,
Positive is courage hope calmness,
Steel nerve knee jerk effort traces,
Negative is lethargy, lies, a careless,
Myopic, fearful, tremble paralyzes,
Better late than never, now or never,
Life ever surrender or safe secure,
Open eyes coin rotates duet suits,
Head or tail apprehension intuits. (4)

Apprehension

Awake, dawn breaks beautifully,
Shake the slumber, wonderful,
Fresh air cool instill all desires,
Sun rises in bridal color inspire,
A new day in the life, wait for opportunity,
Magical thoughts cloud on duty,
A new challenge unknown arrives,
A new person meets a bond that thrives,
New jobs offer a prosperous future,
The new boss understands better,
A new place to travel works invite,
New problem waits for projects to bite,
Complex life, thread with knots,
A miracle unfolds, surface, if buts,
The day riddles solve symphony,
Initial apprehension accompanies,
The day ends, the job is over, happy mind,
Family apprehension does remind, (1)

Evening news telecast views well,
Election trigger expectant swell,
Reclined to sofa watch promises,
Win or loss of vote, luck precise,
Rallies and long speeches excite the public,
Melt in the air always hunt nostalgic,
Leader rises to power on destiny,
Worry and apprehension accompany,
Leaders worry, worry public wait,
Future open avenues of joy later,
Opens job opportunities, grains sold,
Happy youth farmer labors bold,
Avenues fail to open, price rises,
Apprehension happens in surprises,
Picketing rally strike hunt nation,
Disturb life uncertainty in motion,
Leaders appeal to people for harmony,
Shed apprehension to accompany, (2)

Quit television, watch kids in the study,
Class work examination to moody,
Thought of parents entice a result,
Child to pass out with honor most,
Aspiration weaves future rosy await,
Higher study career avalanche gate,
Often smiles dream shadow failure,
Time is the key, and effort indeed assures,
Parents pray reverently and wait for destiny,
Usual let apprehension accompany, (3)

Sleep yet never near rest n think,
Service life will be over a future sink,
Gratuity pension insurance savings,
Secure home, kid's marriage ring,
Insurance cover for health adequate,
Duty for old parent expenses met,
Nightmare is raising costs n finance,
Only the job, a boat on a stormy sea,
Meager savings attract honey bees,
Steal most of savings future looms,
Apprehension accompanies, blooms, (4)

Fast asleep dream watch tomorrow,
Apprehension misses total sorrow,
Equanimity accompanies life is quiet,
Swansong, life sings, gain loss duet. (5)

Arriviste Compose

Silver-spoon never graces life except,
Different world cloud Lord, percept,
The spectacle of pool sprout-life in mud,
Effulgence atomic stage inherits bud, (1)

Equal before creator destinies make,
Destiny molds human minds awake,
Luck fortune myth struggle discover,
Fate, turn sudden imagine manicure, (2)

Never destiny make friends, rich or poor,
Alert dauntless spirit efforts capture,
Stigmas, class vogue, ignominy fade,
Fame illustrious silvery poem pervade, (3)

Brilliant mind lack education puzzle,
Inborn knowledge unfolds soul sizzle,
Unknown, rustic, remote village onus,
Lose untraceable amid nature bonus, (4)

Insatiable appetite, observe assimilate,
Pristine beauty mind metaphor, relate,
Witness poverty, human struggle, pain,
Matchless, indomitable spirits, regain, (5)

Regain, secure life, defeat hunger rise,
Lotus from mud detached lo, surprise,
Mysterious life equates nature n the heart,
Miracle child writes feeling arts impact, (6)

Gifted perception acquires resemblance,
Nature humans match immense trance,
Flows automatic poesy, glitters marvel,
Cross height of mountains art unravel, (7)

Speechless, mesmerized, literate addict,
Golden inks n metaphors hook distinct,
Spread like wind literature across the ocean,
Amazes incredible print applaud, listen, (viii)

Anonymous, village youth socks people,
Name and fame rise to zenith nit simple,
Nation feels proud asset influence script,
Inflame spirits, instant character depict, (9)

Mobilize poem people, save nature earth,
Move stone heart melts serve, new birth,
Golden words inherit n purity of nature,
Spread among people magnetize secure, (10)

Spread amity, compassion, love, dedication,
Incredible appeal brainwashes intimate,
Clear-night-sky, people witness a meteor,
Trailblazer white line etches black-silver, (11)
Short-moment the live sight attracts well,
Flood news accolades of poem lover swell,
Inconspicuous simple villagers enjoy posing,
Creator's mystic touch arriviste compose, (12)

Meteor sketches path shine memory etch,
Memory, write legend imagination fetch,
The arriviste composes manuscripts regal,
Century-after books intoxicate n enthrall. (13)

Arrogance

Imagine a baby cries loud,
Angelic faces anger clouds,
Mother's milk satiates soon,
Worth watching, smiles moon,

The mind is pure, innocent love,
The image of the soul readily absorbs,
Puzzles mind arrogance rule,
Growing age mind is never cool,

Curios look inborn, iron dust,
Human nature magnet most,
The child learns to walk, talk, rest all
Anger, unhappiness, brood recall,

Learn joy, fun, laughter, clapping,
Teen disobeys naughty slaps,
Time yet of ripe on arrogance,
In school, dress, look, fragrance,

Car, Tiffin box, chocolates, gift,
Teacher's care extra widens the rift,
Arrogance germinates bud pink,
A simple look, a poor boy sink,

Arrogance grows faster within the mind,
Humble, innocent, simply blind,
Wealth, glamour, success, growth,
Ignore near, brood, mood shows,

Discipline, rule, obey, falters more,
Warning, penalty, unmindful clear,
Adulthood sees the mind as arrogant often,
Brooding, in mood, anger, depression,

A rich life, name, fame, glamour,
Crowd applause like mad, clamor,
Asset grows fast, gold is a resource,
Path of progress, money outpours,

The mind is no more master to rule,
In the citadel, arrogance dictates cool,
Own world arrogant expects to cower,
A gesture, follower, mentors shower,

The profession is a rainbow of colors,
Art, music, singer, actor, dancer,
Writer, painter, architect, doctor,
Scientist, intellect, pleader, leader,

Business, commerce, media, sport,
Beautiful men, women, legends,
Wealth, power, and fame corrupt the mind,
Absolute status arrogance rekindles,

Arrogance leads to the ego, self, being blind,
Soul, conscience stranger fails to rewind,
Evil rules life, ego controls the character,
Arrogance is flavor corrodes more quicker,

Sadness, depression, tension, anger,
Life sinks in arrogance, none to hear.
Death, reclusion, aloof sad life story,
Erase arrogance and humility, gets the glory,

Arrogance dissolves quickly in care,
Donate most simply wealth to share,
Serve the poor, needy, kids, or sick most,
Valuable in life purified, the ego is lost,

Wisdom character reborn within,
Arrogance melts gentleness shine,
Arrogance tricks mansion, assets,
Two yards brave, a pot of ash to rest,

Lifelong a bed, two yards in need,
Half of life rests, lures greed indeed,
The human need for shelter, food small,
Triggers greed, arrogance, and soul crest fall.

Arrogate Freedom

Watch eagle fly high hovers,
Landscapes all contour lures,
Knows in detail life intimate,
Far off mountains forest wait, (1)

Test freedoms of life interest,
Predator deprive, rest bitterest,
A gorge, cavern, cave, or cliff,
Travels easy nest none to tiff, (2)

Symbol of power strength lit,
Prey weak, wounded no guilt,
A tiny creature on the ground play,
Rabbit beautifully run in gay, (3)

A dark cloud hovers above the well,
Swoops down instantly, quells,
Quell noisy bird silent n fear,
Creatures in groove hide sure, (4)

Rules earth an eagle fascinate,
Arrogates a freedom dominate
Alert on the domain lion roam,
Animal bird lives in freedom, (5)

Nature promulgates joy equally,
Supremacy of king force vocal,
Resound roars in a forest, night,
Horror spreads fast, stays fright, (6)

Contemplate if nature's boon,
Arrogates freedom, fateful doom,
Catch sight of lion eagle mimic,
Human owes endless, yet tragic, (7)

Born free human spirit superior,
Freedom of voice, lifestyle security,
Freedoms to travel the world explore,
Freedom to believe, trust custom,
Freedom to practice will caution, (viii)

Free for equal rights, knowledge,
Equal before people in privilege,
Amazes civilized society, power,
Wealth strength sees rest cower, (9)

Colonial rule abolished freedom,
People in slavery enjoys seldom,
Independence proclaims a plethora,
Freedom, lit life bask in the aura, (10)

Inheritors of exploitations appear,
Eagle in the sky, lions on land sheer,
Human natures ego, selfishness,
Turn predator freedom misses, (11)

Pretentious harmless n arrogates,
Steal voice right equality dictates
Witness revolts, bitter fights hurt,
Society and turbulent progress lost, (12)

Peace security shelter education,
Halt eagle, lions in manifestation,
Dark valleys of anarchy transform,
Rabbit deer resembles spirit, home, (13)

Focus within alarms mind rule,
Alert like eagle ego as lion mull,
Life enjoys peace, happiness, love,
Mind steals all tranquility dissolve, (14)

Spirit in a chain, cruel heart dictates,
Arrogates freedom to blame fates,
Nature balances lion eagle a rest,
Human nature mind capture best,
Mind realize self ruin lit reform,
A seldom act arrogates freedom. (15)

Aspirant

Baffle the morbid worldly pull,
Irresistible attraction life mule,
Pluck a blood rose prick thorn,
Oozing blood scared lo mourn, (1)

That dazzled eyes blinding lit,
Fly burnt wings, death delight,
Born in the twilight less exist,
By dawn, no more, failed to resist, (2)

Intuit intelligence dreamy life,
Worldly illusion allured strife,
Hope Oasis suffocates desert,
Trackless amidst sand impact, (3)

Thirst ambiguous notion drop,
A water drop if quenched hop,
Asks cool breeze shed of trees,
The pond wink lotus surprise, (4)

Spirals desire, luxury comfort,
Blistering hot sun above effort,
Loses sense melting thought,
Paradise vanished, soul fought, (5)

Still wants to live another day,
Probe lotus from mud dismay,
Pristine beauty, fragrant rose,
Yet stinking smell mud shows, (6)

No sign of dirt lotus leaf, sway,
Water bubbles fail to wet and stay,
An aspirant to live, love clean life,
Friendly life honey bees thrive, (7)

Reject anger, greed, jealousy, fit,
Emulate mind lotus leaf treat,
Plays dreary desert animosity,
Lost friendly world to atrocity, (viii)

Revives traveler to a new world,
Hope humans, unity emerald,
Frivolous, treacherous, thought,
Human race selfless life escort. (9)

Asylum Seeker

Look at struggles, for humanity attract,
Dedicates entire life services impact,
Far away from home, family reminds me,
Sense of duty supreme, heart, is kind, (1)

Suffering human skeletal frame sick,
Children, women old alike are at life risk,
Severe malnutrition, lack of food hit,
Find little medicines treatment meet, (2)

Flees huge population for life dictates,
Neighboring-nation all accommodate,
Humanitarian grounds colony grows,
Loss of identity n refugee futures owes, (3)

Nations contribute funds, health care,
Essential shelter food job near share,
World citizens visit monitors provided,
Joins with massive effort time divide, (4)

Nation at conflict cause human loss,
Uncertain futures arise, survive a toss,
Extreme situations are tense and rest seldom
Violence, death, diminishing freedom, (5)

Force plight of women, kids, aged people,
Mass migration happens, feel horrible,
Neither shelter, food, cloth, water,
Open ground harsh weather life fear, (6)

Nations airlift, near seas, allow voyage,
Prime-factor to save people envisage,
Accommodate refuges on alien soils,
Left people's home assets, jobs, and life boils, (7)

Years pass soon, remote return home,
Remote possibilities stare, gruesome,
Local people and sympathies wear thin,
Suffering increases a lot of hope decline, (viii)

Humanity offers adoption citizenship,
World citizen day remembrance whip,
Humans single race sacrifices marvel,
Overseas people gain, right-life unravel, (9)

Surprise human conscience insanity,
Imprisonment, tortures confine priority,
Discrimination hunts every layer neatly,
Ethnic cleansing forced labor discreetly, (10)

Subjugate inhuman rules n helpless,
Art culture security declines distress,
People flee, risk life-hazardous traveling,
Land, air, and water route adopt life, swiveled, (11)

Fate cruelly snatches lives midway notice,
World citizens sympathize, need peace,
Condemns brute forces n united voice,
Accept survivor provide shelter choice, (12)

Modern-times civilization assures help,
Mingle suffering souls as settler shape,
World citizens unite services-awesome,
Asylum reminds hope, homeland seldom, (13)

Destiny snatches identity home cruel fate,
World citizen compassions promulgate.
Savage climate harsh life equal rulers,
Asylum direct agony pain dark colors. (14)

AURA

Polar hypnosis

Neither emphasizes polar aura n prize,
Spectral color sprayed blue skies,
Below horizon expanse white sheet,
Freezing ice desolations aura sweet (1)

Silhouette of the enlightened

Nor project aura of divine concept,
Enlightens aura and picture-perfect,
Nor artificial glow of the human frame,
Glows silhouette aural look blame, (2)

Glows human life

Subtle mystic light aura defuse,
Every human being carries profuse,
Aural presences affect the environment,
Sunken spirit, sad dampen, decent,
Sadness pervades silence, affects all,
Gathering gets sullen laughter fall, (3)

Happiness glows

Peaceful, a sweet home, quiet mind,
Kids make fun, giggle, heart kind,
Incredible family life bondage, love,
Pain, troubles, and tears quick dissolve, (4)

Anger has evil aura color is black

Anger enters the mind, shouts louder,
Smiles fade soon, hunt tense fear,
Aura near the angry mind is darkness,
Spread conspicuous pierce sadness,
Sweet home fizzle fetch hopeless look,
Aural spread cruel, devastate n hook,(5)

The delight of an infatuated heart glow

Visit a dancing parlor mind to music,
Soothing rhythms songs step ecstatic,
Heart sinks in the splendor of consonance,
Aura of the enchanting night, all elegance,
Departed, dearest stop, torture to my heart,
Smiles missing tear dries, life in thirst, (6)

Love song melancholic permeates

A passer-by on a quiet night on a lonely road,
Listen to enchanting music aura broad,

Freeze motion of traveler influence, cool,
Melancholic waves leave tragic, love songs rule, (7)

Prayerful heart shines

Visit a Church, Masjid, or temple for prayer,
Mass prayers colossal infringe love to layer,
Tears in bottom-most heart, joyous mind,
Wishes, pleading acute, friend, loner find,
Human emotions myriads infinite mingle,
Aura of prayer, voices, whispers cripple!
Melts quick emotions intense to calmness,
Tranquil mind self aura in group impress, (8)

Lush green nature glimmers

A journey to nature never overwhelms peace,
Silence a valley, starry skies, moon amiss,
A gentle cool breeze blows, blossoms fragrant,
Summer night nightingale calls aura vibrant,
Heavenly feelings pierce the heart, rapturous,
Aural enigma drifts unreal world curvaceous, (9)

Enigma of childish glint

Ever entice a time with joyful kids' play,
Bright sunshine in meadows, lilies sway,
Swarm around your chest, chat endless,

The aura of children transforms and enchantress,
Angles hurt pain; worries fade for a moment,
Childish goes heart sings, aura mix covalent, (10)

Glitter luxurious life

The last hop let us visit a friend's jewelry shop,
Gold ornaments dazzle the aura envelope,
Visit a showroom for cars most modern,
Gadgets sparkle, entice aura glows stubborn,
Have a relaxed time in a glittering cottage,
Cushions soft, service, travel privilege, (11)

The mystical aura of detachment, the best

Mind intoxicated in affluence aura thick,
Visit cremation ground is quiet yet intrinsic,
A feeling of detachment, time a swindler,
Amorous mind, exotic heart, aura, sober…
Aura is a state of mind, truth realized, rest,
Human silhouette envelops luminous best. (12)

UTUMN ARRIVES

Speechless ma landscape pulsates ecstatic in joy,
Flowers changed blossoms in hues florists enjoy,
Idols profusely garlanded, adored, beautiful,
The red saris vermilion smear face dazzles awful,
White fur flower spread white cover river banks,
Gentle breeze notice nature in wave merrily dance,
Meadows cool springs wait fragrances sweep slow,
Clear skies, white clouds sail abandon sunlit glow,
Lush green scenic nature, smile a bride in gold,
Yellow corn fields pregnant heavy sway in winds bold,
Rural life festive time home busy in cakes sweet disk,
Family converge holiday fever far-flung city crowd risk,
(a)

Humanity sees a year pass submerged in water,
In flood cyclones devastated corn fields in tear,
New Year, big surprise, sweep to shake the heart,
Lock-down Corona across memory confined to home,
Smiles trapped in the quicksand of viral worrisome,
Mother, your loving heart graced, saved most,
A home misses husband, wife, parent, hope lost, (b)

Exhilarate nature is visibly clean and fresh now,
Temple crowding lives feverish prayer bow,
Dusk invites devotees, Temples bright with lamps,
Silently lamps burn, radiate hope, yet tears damp,
Amuses mother incredible bird cattle in mirth,
Untouched to agonies, baby cries at birth,
The heart and emotions surge waves tumultuous,
Less beg mercy mother human deeds preposterous, (c)

What a mind thinks intelligence in spell,
Rosy future new generation sweet dreams trail,
Ancient myth evils perished, Mother was merciless,
Virtue regain again demolish vice, peace clueless,
Arrive, Mother, human spirit expectant feeble,
Decorations pandals festive season simple,
Crowds lighting music dances wishing puja season,
The unique festival year will pass memories, hope won, (d)

Human has two hands, Ma, you offer with ten, strives,
Realize past mistakes and misdeeds, heal lives,
Immense compassion for children, a future,
Wiped pandemic, suffering, a respite to feel secure,
Buffalo demon king metamorphic for lust die,
A virus, no trident, lion, sword, burned third eye, (e)

Fire from burning eyes turns ignorance to ash,
May humanity visualize nurturing nature, alas,
Ego, greed, cruelty, anger, hatred, discrimination,
Heinous demons thrive within mind burns creation,

Love, compassion, care, kindness, simplicity
Devotion, nature care, knowledge sustain,
Tenfold in hands, graceful Mother, season acclaim, (f)

Tears wiped, smiles Mother, moment your presence,
Leave ceremonial parting time trend reminiscence,
A lonely moment meditates on why fail, to imagine,
Warm tears wait for Mother, memories serene.
Blue skies, greens, spring in praying mood fine,
Autumn arrives, mother, it's time… (g)

AVENGED

Tumultuous electric moments,
Aware of the arrival of youth swell,
Unforeseen imaginary spider,
Weaves threads of dream allure,
Like a river to the brim swirling,
Mimic stream of thoughts cling, (1)

Churlish outspoken heart rebel.
Influenced hardened spirit to dwell,
Work harder you work, time short,
Accomplished caps success, effort,
The immensity of determination focus,
Life hardly got averted, not curious, (2)

Spring came, flowers blossomed,
Profusely attractive petals earned,
A gentle breeze swept past limbs,
Tried best to magnetize his heart,
Buzzing swarms off bee joyous,
Spread warmth Sun got mild and sweet,
Played hide and seek with clouds,
Dark clouds turned white monks,
Landscape ornate verdure flowing,

Long grass white furs swayed airy,
Symphony of light and shed pulled, (3)

He averted searching eyes toiled,
Long silent night creepers flowery,
Jasmine invited his spirit Feathery,
The fragrant night river got placid,
Turned silvery under full moon vivid,
Far off a boatman playing his flute,
The ethereal motionless air carried,
Tried the best to molted his heart,
Nature failed in that night dews weep,
Star-studded night leaves dazzled,
Cuckoo sang the song if melancholic,
Bewitchingly attractive seasons failed, (4)

He was burning his midnight lamp,
His youth was precious to grab fame,
Work changes destiny completely,
The world recognizes achievers a lot,
Incredibly popular, his fames, escort,
Luxury comfort gold match wine,
Drink happiness youth felt prime, (5)

Money will make a happy family,
Friends to crowd intent smelly,
Yes, a mighty yes reality happens,
Today his place, prestige sharpen,
From hundred miles people owed,
The disbelief, amused honor showed, (6)

Time hay stealing life stealthily,
Ripping black hair whitish visible,
Wrinkles cover the face recognized,
Feeble eyesight, hearing trouble,
Walking feels difficult with a long stick,
Breathlessness by walking in a park,
Sadly once the youth he is no more,
Twinkling twilight years time unsure, (7)

Sitting on a wooden bench scrutinizing,
Spring visited again decades after,
Astonished, his soul overwhelmed, aura,
Rising crimson sun orange sky lit,
Birds soaring high, chirping gleefully,
Profusely blossoms changed the park,
Spectral hues aflame bright color,
Speechless his young heart no more, (viii)

Throbs missing nerves still and numb,
Soul fails to resonate, respond with aplomb,
Seat here for hours, a statue silent trailed,
Avenged the Spring reminded season failed. (9)

AWKWARD

Surreptitiously searching an anchorage,
The night covered the entire evening electric,
Floated faces long known acquainted,
Glad to meet stumbled with names,

Crept into my mind, memories flashing,
Eyes met eyes in glances delinked,
The quicksand of time memories slipped and lost,
Why tears, the fascinating time only a past,

Failed to find the anchor to the harbor,
Initiate gossip and queries to sweeten a time,
Relation, linked to relatives, far and short,
Relating to life to people in the community,

Smiled tried hard to portray gentleness,
Suavity is an awkward posture cripple,
Lacking the chain of talk name jokes,
Tired of loitering for hours aimlessly,

Missing few who loved seeking vainly,
The occasion was to instill a time,
That I lost whom I adored the most,
A year passed since he departed,

Came praying solemnly for his peace,
Vanished so quickly the reality of crowd,
Awkward to realize time never waits,
It moves, carries many with it for good,
Tiny toddlers were the sight stunningly,
They will be lives for the twenty-first century,
And that will be a different time and world.

Bairn

Stardust in life settles in my lap,
Pain, tears, sleepless nights cap,
Nightlong dream soaked in prayer,
Time graces a bairn no more aspire,

The mind seeks the unknown in life with love,
Cry of bairn, in abode a void dissolves,
The arrival of a newcomer triggers ecstasy,
Meaningless life in a cauldron of fantasy,

Credence to divine grace to family,
Witness baby crawls, plays amply,
Feeding Cairn for his mother is a rare love,
Motherhood glitters nature in throb,

Bairn toddles, giggles noise to Mom,
A sight mother picks up, kisses often,
Pride in heart, empty life, and the home,
Nice, bairn burbles, chuckles own,

Bairn to animals, birds, living forms,
Mother's protection, care in uniform,
A bairn ever grows to be a leader,
Lead humanity in jewel character,

Wisdom incredibly transforms a time,
Leave a legendary flame sublime,
Yet the mind of a Bairn, innocent n pure,
Listens, behold, touches, smiles allure,

Simple trust in mother, known face,
Worth imitating in life, a divine grace,
Trust life is truth, noble mind erases,
Temptation, greed, anger in phases,

The human mind grows complex swell,
Learn deception pretension so well,
Face a bairn, bright angelic look,
Smiles in hugging or licking hook,

Bairn is simple to human life the most,
Searches lifelong divinity ever lost,
Leading a life of a child of god rare,
Essence to realize the creator's gift to share,

Unique is the life of bairn duality none,
Realm with duality with opposite form,
The elusive mind corrodes in time its worst,
Fails to touch the bairn divine mercy most,

Spirit finds the path of rejection in detachment,
Win its delusion mind surrenders in attack,
Surrender to purity, truth, trust, and love,
Sinful life, dark mind quick absolve,

Puzzle in creation finer a bairn, a soul,
Never saw in life except for the mother a goal,
Rarest mother, her love, care, blood,
Her milk, time, nightlong awake episode,

The sight of a Bairn in the back of the mother, sweet,
In works, field walks of life, her toil greet,
Never asks for gratitude, applause in life,
Ripe age, the mother changes a bairn, precise,

Bairn arrives in deathlike pain from the womb,
Mother tolerates all abject least to succumb,
Divine speechless at human selfishness,
Mother, as a bairn, in age rots in loneliness,
No one to feed, care for, or a sleepless night,
In Sickbed, the wonderful creator forces us to fight!

Bait

Eon hunger of mind insatiable dwell,
Living being flies, runs, swims n trails,
The pull for life instincts survive only,
Food is not only hunger, desire yet truly,

Desire infinite in mind prowls to quench,
Prevention through bait entrap to fetch,
Plants, animals, creatures found in a trap,
Birds and aquatic life get caught, bait caps,

Carrion smells a mile away, bait tricks quick,
Mind blinds alertness rare is inquisitive,
Elephants fall to pits, the tiger in cages roar,
Bird for grain in net, bait hook fish to sore,

Flower, leaf with sweet smell liquid bait,
Insects trapped by plants, deception trek,
Life baits n deceiving minds, captures, quick,
In cages or death, living beings end tragically,

Humans do face bait entices offer in a trick,
Concession in the price for-good hides a risk,
Saving money assets growing more,
People seek advice to invest bait do allure,

Promises and data are deceptions, bait to loot,
Broken home, life shattered, lust is the root,
Clarion on the job, overseas life, travel in Hoot,
Bait fails alert mind notice cheats lurk,

Overnight young life loses all future sunk,
Ruler lays bait people elect in plain trust,
Commodities free gift bait future is lost,
Promotion in career bait, surrender reason,

Rejection of compromise tagged as treason,
A faceless sweet voice lures an intimate message,
Spies hunt secrets, bait blackmail cleavage,
Bait is female lure rules bends save crime,

Wine, riches, and asset bait ensure compromise,
Corrupt-mind breeds bait undercover ruin,
Anarchy spread the pretension plenty are twins,
The essence of humanity, the righteous path, adheres to,

Gait is quicksand in temptation acts eraser,
Life, in principle, is a test for a walk with thorns,
Corrupt escapes with booty taunt a lorn,
Bait act of evil for the detached spirit with a goal,

Emancipation, a penance, guides a soul,
Society gets cleansed progress manifest,
Character ensures peace awareness crest,
Where bait promotes violence n arson,

A corrupt mind ignores willfully, reason,
Character-of-evil digs a grave, bait waits,
Credence to culture civilizes life in traits.
The human instrument is intelligent, wisest,
Modern times bait survives nicely infest,
War is neither with people nor with other nations,
War is with mind clean life n corruption

Barricade

Unruly child disobeys orders,
Prejudice, I treated all along,
Injustice for controlling children,
Allowed me to discover, I felt curious,

Picturesque world attracting,
Enough to trap mind things allure,
Enough to capture heart beautiful,
Revolted disciplines, barricades,

No, to see, refuse to hear, speak,
Refuse food outside, taste,
Ignore words touching, caring,
Elders taught me, warned, cautioned,

Discrimination is essential for life,
Barricade external wind, destroy,
Pollute your heart, poison your mind,
What it says is the truth; utter lies,

Fabricated for belief by innocent,
Unscrupulous, ignorant, soul fertile,
Planting seeds of poisoned fruit is easier,
Watch, read, think, and consult everything,

Dear child, rely on elders, parents,
Teachers, best educators focus right path,
Unknown people, their advice placate,
Best ignore, least react, a little infuriate,

Cyberspace massive universe message,
Crisscross the globe instantly,
Try to establish a community group,
Sympathetic, believing, brainwashed,

Train through Internet violence sabotage,
Establish an imaginary kingdom by force,
Gun speaks, knife blade,
Gunpowder explodes, killing the opposition,

Expand, and circulate myth sacred,
Spare your life for the cause, salvage,
Golden paradise waits, fairy welcomes,
Sacred interprets the cause, war brutal,

Myth only a faith, political system,
Myth is an evil practice, immortality,
Myth is race, pure, supreme blood,
Rest people are destined to be subjects,

Resisted to be conquered, mass killing,
Myth is the dominance of one people,
Myth is color, caste, language, region,
Segregate people under the barricade,

Unequal, illegal, discriminate,
Barricade people from the right people,
Myth is supreme, the truth, rest false,
Arrest defying spirits suppress,

Laugh today no more stay a child,
Learned civilized society and fallacy,
True, education can light upon evil,
Can distinguish huge crowds barricaded,

Close group, believing calling rest impure,
Fit for massacre conversion subjugate,
Existence for decades, centuries, old,
Education can not cure cancerous growth,

Laugh today, my parent alarmed,
By my questions, get silent,
Lo… never ask these questions, wrong,
Keep aloof from such people, never listen,

Barricade yourself, dear child,
Humanity is different than segregation,
The division is inherent, evil, and noble,
Interpretation depends upon people,

They practice, keep live culture,
Barricades the heart before being captured,
Barricade your mind, thought to entrap,
Barricade confines my soul, is self-built,
Fear contamination if you cross,
It was the voice of my mother, once warning.

Be Human

Unearth mysterious eventful realm,
Scintillates domestic animal qualm,
Hypnotizes masculine limbs strong,
Six-feet tall scales Everest, tell long, (1)

Two-footers cross oceans and continents,
Adventure, fuel blood, boldly resilient,
Magnetic charisma speech anchors,
Golden hand pen literature harbors, (2)

Mysterious mind unique n universe,
Inner cosmos, knowledge's converse,
Pair of sight sound collect message,
Interprets the human mind, not courage, (3)

Animal spirits refined food n shelter,
Procreate in privacy enemy, the fear,
Separate humans from animals naked,
Covers body immaculately, acts wicked, (4)

Shrewdest, living species rules, earth,
Perplex behavior tag caste clan birth,
Intelligence differs worst rest, animal,
Divide birth color nit gender unequal, (5)

Voracious eater, digest tree, mountain,
Quenches thirst, drinks rivers, ocean,
The earth appears to be a small shelter quiet,
Search, cosmos planets settle despite, (6)

Loves naming self social animal craze,
Inner instinct selfish, cruel act savage,
Death fears the savagery of human-mind,
Demonic nature exhibit massacre find, (7)

Brutality unthinkable alter, landscape,
Living beings face extinct n no escape,
Human race depiction is not all horrible,
Lotus in muddy water glows incredibly, (viii)

A dark world under bright sun and ignorance,
Manifest savagery sacrilege lit elegance,
The silvery light of the moon floods the night,
Burns little lamp, darkness inner mind light, (9)

Illusive realm corrode character nature,
Attachments to desires sensation savor,
Awakens a mind, realizes a goal of sojourn,
Short live opportunity huge less mourn, (10)

The inner lamp reveals universal truth neatly,
Love compassion care summon, discreet,
Nonviolent, humble, and friendly exhibit well,
Trust benevolence serves sympathy, fuel, (11)

Human, gift of creator domestic animal,
Civilization eons witness miracle survival,
Depress seasons of bitter war n carnage,
Bloodthirsty human roams nit sacrilege, (12)

Brick of civilization nation, roots family,
Husband, wife, and children welcome, wisely,
Happiness, laughter, bondages coagulate,
Paradise on earth sweet home a magnet, (13)

Attracts humans, immense pull quit, war,
Be human mind is wild nature is never far!
At day sun, at night moon in mud lotus,
Be Human means family life is enormous. (14)

Beacon Of Hope

When darkness spreads, life searches,
Ignorance opaque sight, fear lurch,
Poverty, sickness, vices, blind rule,
Suffering, pain, and death prevail cool,

Bitterest fights, hatred, and jealousy grow,
Violence, evil practices, wild show,
Nation for century rots under slavery,
Lack of education, life bleak and unsavory,

Jobless youth vulgar, crude mind,
Unmarried girl burden brute remind,
Old age sick seek to escape for good,
Parents with large offspring in wood,

A canvas of society painted black, if true,
A beacon of hope, inventions surreal,
The new millennium, a beacon of light,
Life at the bottom sees a tunnel, bright,

Earthen oven, dry wood smoke blight,
Replaced with biomass oven in flame,

Replaced with solar panel, solar oven,
The rural cottage, now brighter, television,

Women welfare telecast skills reason,
Kids learn education about air, wave,
Farmers learn cultivation to save,
Clean gas, hot plate solar is electric,

Rural female life in heath magic,
Toilet culture, brick home alters,
Beacon of hope for lifestyle betters,
The modesty of women in sweet home,

Skilled in domestic products own,
Own handsome in food, spices, toys,
Stitch clothes, cosmetics, art voyages,
Savings able children, school, college,

Girls of generation progress in knowledge,
Biogas fuels, compost need fields,
Water harvest feed betters yield,
Means of rural scene richer fine,

The inroad of heath care cattle shine,
Beacon of hope gains fizzle darkness,
Rural women in free scope reckless,
A nation's backbone farmers, women,

Awakens freedom, bondage in the chain,
The chain was behind the door for females,

A chain was illiteracy for kids swells,
A chain was sickness, lack of treatment,

A chain was vagaries of climate bent,
A chain was elements devastate ruin,
Beacon of modern help broke n win,
Bondage disappear for women folk,

Beacon of reforms village girl mock,
Beacon of education, skill alter soon,
Beacon of silver light, sizzles full moon,
The new millennium corona specter is bleak,

Locked down cities, roads, life pinprick,
Hospitals overflowing with sick intense,
Modern care, the prowess to cure pretense,
Clueless calamities swindle a year,

Education halts, halt industry near,
Blocked travels, suffered export most,
Progress of nation under lock share lost,
Darkness wraps the future, the human mind,

Paralyzes escape instinct beacon reminds us,
The populace is disciplined in the mask, clean,
Distancing, saving crowd, domestic rinse,
Vaccine, exercise, fresh air, nature,

Forestation, preservation of water,
Beacon of hope potent counter well,
Beacon of cure, numbers recover swell,
Beacon of confidence nation roll,
Beacon of joy; wait for peace, happiness prowl.

BEATITUDE

Rise of the reason
Past the tree of mind grow
Spreads branches of thoughts
Bearing actions share in draught

That fills life from birth to death
And bearing flowers and fruits
A blossom spreads a fragrance or foul smell
And generate further actions to infect

Osmosis rises to many more branches
A surge in leaves of memories
Fall in time deep into deep depth
Of the ocean of the subconscious mind

Reason with immense light dispels
All thoughts to see the dualities,
Illusions n pretensions of Maya
Focus reason on eternal truth,

Imperishable deathless and non-dual
Ever shining overhead
With the brilliance of thousands of sun
And all-pervading within the spirit

Nothing in the external world is permanent
As a reality, it dies with time,
The inner quest to a universe,
Traverse between the branches of thoughts

To a state where there is silence
Infinite thoughts subdued
Intellect and intuition surrendered,
The soul bathed in the rays of truth

Overhead and all its conceptions,
Faith belief attachment melts
To the awakening in beatitude
Feels it's time to depart to that world,

His abode waits as always.
Mother with infinite love and compassion,
You have so much love n care...
The Lord is in me,

And the Lord is in your reflection,
Breaths are feeble
The frame is still like a rock
The silence is music in my heart,

Solitude serene in mind,
Thought clouds beyond the horizon,
Stars are shining dazzle
The turmoil of life falls silent,

All the pains and suffering erase
Listen to the unstuck bells
Love radiant plunge into the beatitude
Rains pour down without water

Rivers are streams of light
How could I ever express
How speechless I feel
To revel in such vast ecstasy

Of the land, of quietude
The landscape of peace n bliss
This is the music
Of soul and the Supreme meeting,

Of all grief fade dissolved
This is the music
That transcends all oscillate
The beatitude permeates the state of mind.

Beguiling Mind

The beguiling mind is a beehive,
It entraps life, wise survives,
Blind ruler if mind, the body obeys,
Limbs act to wishes life misses,

Ever clean is the mind, pure divine,
The essence of the elusive realm decline,
Tame a beguiling mind is a mirage,
Patience, practice is lifelong courage,

The bondage of life is in birth and death,
Liberation is guarded by the mind n in-depth,
Mind beguiled divine, after golden deer,
The Sita got kidnapped, deceived by a fake seer,

Life of the king in truth, his mind was in service,
The weakest moment mind beguiling, for dice,
King lost his kingdom and his wife,
Eon's messages of lives in ruin are clear,

Ruins mind human life, beguiling steer,
A power can travel in the realm in no time,

The mind finds itself imagining fine,
Can penetrate the wall, rise on the hill,

Can dive depths of the ocean, dream reveal,
Beguiling mind deceit spirit as ego,
The mind has charms of temptation, desire,
Greed, anger, lust, hatred, evil inspires,

A captured thought as clouds cover,
Soul and conscience feel insecure,
Life ignores wisdom, inner dictates,
Humanity serves the mind, thus displays,

Love, compassion, care, sharing in life,
Mind in selfish urge, it acts as a knife,
At times men are wise and pretend to be well,
Genuine, decent, honest mask mind dwells,

Survive dice till recent addicts swarm,
Lottery, chit fund, share, few pockets warm,
All are slaves-of-the mind allure overnight rich,
A time comes, soul ruins beguiling ditch,

Never humanity learn from a beggar,
Often, a slave-of-the mind loses cry in hunger,
Mind beguiling fox human to drink or drug,
In hallucination, keep mute a wooden log,

The selfish bent of mind children quit their parents,
Shelter home, peddler old rot decent,
Fair prices, discounts, and prizes beguile cool,
Teens, young and old, get trapped like a fool,

A slave-of-mind rise in power leads,
A cruel fate for people beguiling bleeds,
Nature beguile creatures to trap n kill,
A flower traps insects and scents to thrill,

A musk deer seeks fragrance in the forest,
Beguile the scents of musk in its head, rest,
Beguiled flies by a light, jump to fire,
Traps for rats, animals' hunger desire,

Man sets a trap to catch a rat in a puzzle,
The mind-beguiling picks, tries, fizzles,
Soul n mind both live in self in life,
The soul is deathless, the mind perishes right,

Soul whispers through conscience pure,
Mind beguiling intoxicates heart, allures,
Self ceases credence acts as sick, no cure,
Detox beguiling mind fails by vain procedure,

Cleanse in sacred water, pure, divine nature,
Bathing in the Ganga, worshiping an idol,
Mind the same smiling within the soul in torture,
The only way to serve the needy selflessly n to share,

Live life simply in love and heart to care,
Love silence, solitude, focus consciousness,
Detach from desires, practice faithfulness,
Surrender every action in mind to the divine,

A lifetime purifies the mind with simple and serene,
Beguiling-mind obstructs thousand-fold,
Inner trust in the creator holds the fort,
Mortal frame bleeds, writhes in pain,
Entrapment of mind, effort in vain,
Enslaved to conscience mind, transforms,
The secret of the realm beguiles its own reform.

Being Woman

Inscrutable expressions guise smile,
Obscure, inconspicuous nit lifestyle,
Behind veil eyes dazzle n unspoken,
Soul radiates love, river-of-emotion, (1)

Embodiment endurance, less friction,
Humble immaculate neat expression,
Tender heart fragile often scintillate,
Eye messages million-word intimate, (2)

Passionately devoted, serve sincerely,
Lifelong shoulder responsibility fully,
Little complaints, grudge hurt obscure,
Walk, wholeheartedly share life allure, (3)

Trustful, absorbs agony, worry, fear,
Symbolize ocean-of-pain notion tear,
Her husband knows details n erases,
Separation tortures, presence craze, (4)

Conjugal lives nourish vital strength,
Meet challenges n troubles at length,
Unparallel understanding of life beliefs,
Holds home family wife's nit beehive, (5)

Melodious song couple sings unique,
Love blossoms, end marriage ecstatic,
Adulthood, girlfriend seem-hypnotic,
Discover, share hopes mood pathetic, (6)

Dawn, afternoon, and dusk meets enthrall,
Endless gossips mix emotion n trivial,
Acknowledge solace exhibit, girlfriend,
Indiscipline young heart tamed amend, (7)

Induce focus guide her love hint tips,
Deception breaks her, nature weeps,
Discipline-automatic smiles are precious,
Husband establishes in life n famous, (viii)

Romantic life, fruitful marriage graces,
A husband becomes a father, impress.
Mesmerizes time n life, unforgettable,
Moments, watch child, joy detectable, (9)

Unable to search word overwhelm nit,
Wife, being a woman graceful n exhibit,
Flood emotions, grateful for her husband,
Her gifts beautiful baby magic-wand, (10)

The wife becomes mother, the news is good,
Unique n unparallel the motherhood,
Her loyalty, askance prefers, too little,
Expresses love and admiration, her smile, (11)

Her watchful eyes help n walk the baby,
Astonish first-teacher to kid n hobby,
Ripe age twilight years all mysterious,
Serve her love watch health cautious, (12)

Healthy physically, mentally n secure,
Her savings in secrecy, future, assure,
Home maker, decorum docile ovation,
Morning walk together excite occasion (13)

Listen to good news, grandchild visitor,
Being a woman maintains world superior,
Wife, being a woman, her gift mesmerizes,
Moments becoming a father hypnotize. (14)

Believed

In front, across the street, a house,
Double-storied but empty, totally,
Lives the lady decent and mannered,
Advanced in age but alone living,

Her husband expired a few years ago,
In front of our bedroom window,
On the balcony, Madam used to sit,
Morning rays fall on the verandah,

She used to read a newspaper on a chair,
A lady servant, a driver maintains,
Rarely goes out to work in the city,
Cordial relationship Knew her well,

Her only child is at a foreign shore,
Completed study, married and works,
Settled happily corresponds often,
Feeling sad and concerned for her,

She is not pulling well and feels helpless,
Intermittently I enquired about her health,

She was bedridden for the last few days,
Attending her with medicines, food,

She told intimated her son to come,
Intimated her son on his arrival,
In the morning, she is on her balcony,
Watching desperately, son's arrival,

Knew she was sick and concerned,
Her white saree was cleanly covered,
Sitting on a chair on the edge, attentive,
The clock rolled quickly to afternoon,

She was sitting there, quietly calm,
Looking at every bus, car, pedestrian,
Her gaze was telling a million words,
The evening is only past, feared and looked at,

She was still sitting there composed,
Disturbed, she was sick open air facing,
I realized she was serious, if not rested,
Went to her home and goaded her a lot,

To take rest and sleep her body needs,
Socked by her reply, she told me,
She used to wait for him for hours,
Her child used to visit college return,

Quite late, he arrives home to meet her,
Never could her child know a fact,

For hours used to stand near the door,
Wait till her child returns back,

Remain alert till he goes to his bed,
Morning bus her son picks up,
She used to stand at the door,
Till the bus vanished from view,

She never fails to get aware of his time,
Leaves automatic, everything to stand,
Till he is in sight, takes a long breath,
Eager for his arrival, she wanted,

His first sight of coming home today,
Surprised by now, she silenced me,
Continue to sit on the balcony too late,
She slept on her chair, felt tears,

Went back to my house, greatly worried,
Her son arrived in the morning and saw,
Dashed to her home and found her unconscious,
We admitted her to a hospital quickly,

I told her son everything in detail,
He was shocked, speechless, then crying,
Believed her mother, never lose her,
A few days after Madam returned home,
Packing her baggage with her son to travel,
I congratulated her travel with her son,
She replied she believed he would return.

Bemoan Beatitude

Ultimate aspiration emblem,
Pictures mirage, soul blame,
Moon, never descend touch,
Desire lovelorn heart search, (1)

River of tears disobey control,
Agony flood miss ocean call,
Ocean of hope passion loom,
Beatitude, river merge boon, (2)

Tear of agony meets passion,
Fulfills the human heart beacon,
Beacons, happiness overflow,
Family friend n relative glow, (3)

Parents wish a child's marriage,
Askance hideous couple haze,
Wanton desire for a child clip,
Clip wings of conjugal life nip, (4)

Man's ego holds back tear test,
Tumult surge hurt mute best,
Wife open, expose ruins bitter,
Askance acute rot frame litter, (5)

Humanity faces an urge allure,
Child, grand-kid hunt future,
Before conceiving kid worship,
Prayer Lord endless, do weep, (6)

Fate, fortune, luck friend-less,
Want acute moon to miss the stress,
Mysterious world surprise nit,
Family with kid noisy discreet, (7)

Sibling number exceeds prayer,
God's curios play lets kids rare,
Never did I question childless life,
Smile only mask, guises strife, (viii)

Strife, emotion, thought, relate,
Hunger for sweet kid frustrate me,
Draw canvas of the dawn wait,
Cruel human graceful, negate, (9)

Deny outright birth of a child,
Read murder infanticide wild,
Prevent birth, daughter curse!
Dowry, womanhood if source? (10)

Illegitimate child innocent earn,
Add orphanage one parent con,
Wed legitimate child grow nice,
Divorce soon, parents practice, (11)

My way or high way roam child,
Beguile life in the womb blame wild,
Savage humans pray Lord to insult,
Lord's love beast nature assault, (12)

Untold, ocean of tears, not hunger,
Endless, a sea of tears, Lord Fear,
Child image of Him innocence all,
Malnutrition illness illiteracy toll, (13)

Neglect human future ruins roots,
Bemoan beatitude hacks your foot.
Questions conscience of morality,
Bemoan beatitude checks mortality. (14)

BENEFACTOR

Motherland

Motherland nourishes a billion lives,
Immense contribution joy thrives,
Great are river water underneath pour,
Her milk, sacred water child savors,
Soil river basin confluences, fertile,
Bountiful, her hand feeds versatile,
Feed enough billion-plus, children,
Flood-depleted rain rarest frighten,
Glaciers feed annual, river swollen,
Overwhelm harvester crops, golden,
Rice wheat grain cotton oilseed jute,
Vegetables surplus peasant execute,
Motherland is rich in minerals, plentiful,
Gold, silver, copper, iron, coal, oil pool,
Sunshine kiss icy peaks, gold crown,
Vast green forest lake lagoon, renowned,
Motherland, the most beautiful, insecure,
Disenchanted kid, bereft benefactor, (1)

Mother

Sadly, the benefactor, mother pleads,
Home food cloth education job leads,
Affluence knowledge experience a skill,
World acclaims generous genius will,
Highest education in health n business,
Large pools of technical wing impress,
Enable citizens to prosper n world travel,
Freedom, democracy, equality, unraveling,
Never before the motherland united ruin,
Fractured fragments kingdom queen,
Ignorance of poor sick children or a slave,
Century generation none help n save,
United with freedom stronger nation,
Peace, prosperity, cohesion, in motion,
Bondage slavery discrimination none,
Free travel job business, family, home,
Free education, health benefactor love,
The scholarship and soft loan are all to resolve,
Education, technical, medical, services,
Motherland bereft benefactor distress, (2)

Dedicated to land

Distress educated leave the shoreline most,
Impress overseas nations, careers lust,
Lost wisest children motherland looks,
Development industry medical all hook,
Powerful absolute societies corrupt most,

Decency, serving all, sharing care and love lost,
Love for benefactor gratitude perishes,
Violence, arson, insult, anger, blemishes,
Superfluous grain production, ever rot,
Lethargy, irresponsibility, rule millers cost,
Destroys hard labor of peasant regular,
Strike non-production block in particular,
Motherland in sock her children desert,
Least of love, to serve rebuilds thrust,
Motherland laments millennium to suffer,
Donate your lives to the bereft benefactor. (3)

Beneficence

Life manifests glorious existence,
Plant all bewitching beneficence,
Nature serenely mesmerizes the mind,
Plant life perplex flower fruit find,
Flowers fragrant steal heart color,
Honey bee steals from all flowers,
Garland gift pack of flower allure,
Divine to humans use love n pure,
Tree-laden ripe fruit, sweet n sour,
Watch, get wild, all tasty fruit savor,
Few fruits are colorful, never eatable,
Bird insect animals eat, relatable,
Mango, guava, jackfruit, grape apple,
Bewitching beneficence and simple,
A thousand fruits nourish intense,
Steals heart bewitching beneficence, (1)

Cocoanut palm cashew, beetle nut,
Peanut groundnut allures walnut,
Seeds rich in nourishment are all picked,
Human, animal creature bird seek,
Paddy wheat plants feed life,

Mustard cocoanut palm oil refined,
Succulent sauce flavors sweet fruits,
Edible oil aromatic frying pan noise,
Hunger greedily savors enamor poise,
Rice, bread, vegetable curry, fried mix,
Decorate the dining table, invite mind fix,
Potato, eggplant, cabbage, cauliflower,
Carrot radish pea onion red pepper,
Ginger garlic mushroom cucumber,
Tomatoes, corn, pumpkin, curry clear,
Much more fruit n vegetable drinks,
Vegetarian diet, hungry heart sinks,
World over, humanity gratefully eats,
Bewitching beneficence plants treat, (2)

A long list of fruit flower seeds, serve,
Greedy mind eraser human unnerve,
Burns forest fire, cut wood, clean field,
Cities road industry expands no yield,
Fertile polluted polyester-coated earth,
Bread, rice, vegetables, miss, erases mirth,
Poisoned soil earth vomit venom worst,
Fruit garden water bodies vanish most,
Barren field hot climate rain is remote,
Wind blow soil devastation is wrought,
No more green forest cover stands well,
A dry riverbed brook fountain once dwell,
Sweltering heat tortured soul cry aloud,
Miracles manifest lone soul plants proud,

Lifetime effort alone worked hard water,
The forest stand bird sings green color,
Fruit vegetable grows once again lesson,
Beware of bewitching beneficence won. (3)

Benefit

Have ever a spirit faced hunger,
Begged for a morsel of food, staring,
The pain, severe than death etched,
Remind the time scar of the past,

Tears dried long ago, lips parched,
Unruffled matted hair little oily,
The dirty cloth torn at places sadly,
Shame for a life left brutally ago,

Neither faced humiliation nor insult,
His shrunken eyes look at the bystander,
Unmindful of the reaction, extended hand,
Empty palms a few coins he received,

Little reacted, aimlessly focused,
Whom he is calling talking interrupted,
Scolding someone nowhere seen,
Sleeping on the road divider cemented,

Merciless sun blistered his skin,
Failed to recognize the heat seats,
Knew well that people can provide some,
Maybe bread, leftover plates of food,

Some money, mercifully some water,
Rain has arrived pouring rain,
Does not know he may catch a cold,
Soaked to the bone, begging for a sight,

The traffic was thick, passing fast,
Nobody looked at him, squatted,
In the middle of the road, vehicles too,
Speeding past him blaring horn,

Crossing near him less bothered,
Civilization knows the value of time,
Opportunity is missed and never seen in life,
That moment fetched huge benefits,

Mountain of cash gold lot of assets,
Secured life wealth guarantees well,
Magnetic prosperity status face crowd,
They plead for help, beg mercy, obey,

Surrender to whims least bother to act,
Can loot, cheat, make blunders happily,
Wanted favor from the powerful, kneeled,
Give him the order to perform but help,

His son for a job, his wife treated, continues,
He wants a house, acres of land, a shop,
Endless requests touching feet quickly,
Get a bundle of cash promises, of course,

Vanish like thin air all of sudden,
Lock stock and barrel plundered socked,
Touch the feet acquired instantly,
None can challenge men shadowy,

Vanish from visibility mysteriously,
Fear grips lost everything outright,
The law of the land out of reach mockery,
A family of decent having home children,

He once objected to grabbing,
Knocked the door of the court bitterly,
Protested against unseen forces angrily,
He survived lost his family sadly,

The public reacted, consoled him, forgot,
He is changed to an unknown face in the street,
A beggar in the street walking madly,
He knew, lost his home, and family instantly,

Never harmed anyone in life innocent,
Scolding someone looking up angrily,
Passerby ridicule interpret gimmickries,
Everything I know about his neighbor,

Hardly can dare to touch him to help,
Found him senseless on the road,
Called a shelter home, paid dues,
The story didn't end recovered,
Got benefits for those below the poverty line.

Benevolence

The Almighty

Born on soil wish O' Benevolent,
Forgot prayer blessed birth decent,
Devoid of pleasure, love, joy, all void,
Eternal afloat birth, death let avoid,
Wishes soul happy life enjoys love,
Deathless undefined meet dissolve,
Golden honeycomb earth so elusive,
Manifold entrance wait for exit deceive,
Intoxicate earth life sensation thrill,
Soul forgets home nature lot reveal,
Sun moon star, studded night day,
Animals, plants, fish, birds, humans, play,
Benevolent the Lord allow soul sojourn,
Myriad lives journey departure none,
Lifecycle infinite soul traverse being,
Life benign benevolence cycles wing, (1)

The Earth and mother

Earth and mother nature nurtures the soul,
Motherly womb shelter months' goal,
Feeds the baby his own body nourishes well,
Mother's benign benevolence n dwell,
Mothers milk care protection is infinite,
Baby grows in time young lives delight,
Gift of motherland benevolence act,
Fresh air pure, water, food, rest intact,
Sweet home shelter dress well covers,
Blizzard thunderstorm cyclone hovers,
Mother earth protects animals, birds, life,
Creature insects and plant all tolerate alive,
Allows the growth of multiple manifestations,
Mountain river lake valley forest field,
Benign benevolence nature, ever yield (2)

The Motherland

Fortunate motherland, bow to your soil,
Bountiful grain fields nourish son toil,
The buoyancy of ancient culture inherit,
Peace, prosperity, and cohesion all exhibit,
Glaciers feed rivers, mountain ranges,
Mighty rivers and long shoreline edges,
Tropical forest greenhouse fertile land,
Plural community unite family brand,
Inherit temple fort palace monuments,

Wisdom millennium rich, documents,
Unique oriental look beautiful mother,
Benign benevolence heart n protector, (3)

The seer

Fertile faith belief practice ritual dwell,
Prophet seer monk guides divine swell,
World faiths merge ancient religions rich,
Disciple erases ignorance guru bewitch,
Selfless services for people enlighten,
Resurrect realized master soul brighten,
Cleanse greed, jealousy, anger, hatred, rot,
Love, compassion, humility, sympathy lot,
Amidst violence threat arson life suffer,
Benign benevolence faith is a true healer. (4)

Benumbed

There was a knock opened the door,
A postman in front money order,
She signed yes and received the cash,
Only a thousand notes she counted,

Closed the door and sat on the bed,
Tearful lost in thought for an hour,
She was without food for a few days,
Got respite to pay for groceries,

For weeks she bought couldn't pay,
The shop owner was kind enough,
But that was the end of goods on loan,
There is not a morsel of food, rice,

Paid back the money to buy a few,
Essential items, ration for weeks,
Small house, two rooms her home,
End of a street blind alley narrow,

She lives alone with her son abroad
Her husband met an accident,

Couldn't survive shattered her,
Only earning member wife and son,

Left suddenly mourned family,
She worked as a domestic servant,
Stitching lady's garments at home,
Her son studied at school passed,

Scholarship and study loans helped,
Completed higher education degree,
Overseas career invited him and job,
He stays abroad for years,

Left his mother alone no contact,
The lady is sick no more can work,
Meager money from stitching managed,
Medicine costs bending her back,

Failed to contact her son no reply,
Settled to her plight, clueless lonely,
Poverty disconnected her from rest,
She had in-laws, her brothers wealthy,

But life checkmated her links, sadly,
Her life is a forgotten world separated,
The dark lane neighbors feel pity,
Provide compassionate help limit,

Surprisingly brittle fate lo fractured,
Her son she lost contact with presumed,
That he is lost to her too, fate plays,
The white patches on black hair,

Eyes moist, heavy eyebrows, face pale,
Tender frame weak and sick often,
Knew her life at fag end of the story,
Knew the end feared to arrive abruptly,

She may collapse on the ground,
Reluctant to pray Lord smiles a bit,
Press her lips with your teeth, hold her,
Rejected crying shedding tears,

She has done her duty for the child,
The remnant of her beloved living,
Secured, she served her husband,
May his soul be happy, his son stable,

Wait to quit the Blind Alley unable,
Socked to get a money order surprised,
Confused puzzling his son remembers,
Remember his mother in the world,

Living still hand to mouth lost hope,
Can no way contact him, she thought,
Felt tears allowed to flow, cried a little,
It happened, and she knew it would happen,

Discovered in a hospital bed critical,
She fell, got a head injury, fortunate,
Neighbors helped to hospital kindly,
Her son is back home with family,

Returned and accepted a job here,
He took his mother home, relieved,
Benumbed his mother looking,
Her hopes were lost, but she wanted to live...

Beseech

Disturbed, wake up by now alerted,
Who rings a bell in the dead of night,
The temple nearby has a bell hanging,
Pervades the chimes incessant ringing,

Submerged in thoughts analyzed,
Why do humans beg for mercy, a stone idol,
Breaks a dawn crowds gather every day,
Scented sticks, oil lamps lit permeate,

Vibrant divine feeling alive trust swell,
Aspirations countless family life dwell,
Children to educate succeed efficiently,
Parents, tearful pleadings tell murmur,

Young girl with flower fruit sweets,
Oil lamps scented sticks to offer piously,
Her tender heart believes Lord living,
Idol listens to her askance and fulfills,

Lord, give me a handsome, decent man,
Wealthy, educated, kind, and loving,
His family will be compassionate too,
Grace her Lord for such a wedding nicely,

The octagenarian is crying, bitterly gasping,
Uncontrolled his pain, his son missing,
No information alien land helpless,
Begging mercy for his son to return intact,

Folded hands standing for hours,
Sobbing the sight infecting others,
Here is another woman middle age,
Banging her head on the steps hard,

Why Lord, you have stolen my husband,
Not too aged, only earning member,
Her angry look at the idol disturbing,
Shouting loudly, why you are cruel,

How I shall feed three children tell me,
Forced to live to keep my kids,
Got unconscious people attending,
No reaction of the Lord, Idol mute,

On many occasions, I cried before Him,
How many humans trust you, Lord,
Love immensely hope protection,
Surprised, sad news shatters them,

Still, pray for mercy worship in life,
Every stratum of human life confides,
Infinite human desire heart passionate,
No records of how many were fulfilled,

Seen temple agog with ceremony,
Happy occasion festivals jubilation,
Seen smiling faces, laughter, dancing,
People believe Lord listens to functions,

God knows impassionate or interested,
His metallic eyes are fixed fewer winks,
Whether human life is his play, he knows,
Seen lives intoxicated with devotion,

Sing and dance day-long feasting,
Lord is with us and helps us believe,
Wake up alerted enough and anxious,
The bell was ringing resounding bedroom,

Went to the nearby temple and found out,
The accident happened, a few were killed,
Only son of a man wounded critically,
He was ringing the bell of the temple,
Let Lord hear him beseech his son's life,
His faith was far greater than the divine.

Bestowed

Beautiful my house roof concert,
Brick walls, plastic paint coated,
Bedroom floor carpeted soft win,
Cushions on the mahogany bed,

Pillows foamed luxuriant living,
Disturbed past midnight, wake up,
Fully awake at a loss, felt clueless,
Vanished sleep, curious, surprised,

On the balcony discovered heavy rain,
Lightning and thunder hail storms,
My shivered spine got wet instantly,
Back to my bedroom, consequently,

Rest on my bed, listening to noises,
Heavy shower shuddered heart,
Strike thought devastatingly now,
In front of the house, a thatched hut,

Knew well paddy straws destroyed,
A family man, wife, three children,

Water must be poured into the room,
Soaked to the bone, get tortured,

The thought was sickening discovered,
Felt fortunate my bedroom was safe,
Water cannot penetrate wind,
The warmth, blanket, air-conditioned,

How lucky my life than people saw,
Homes like that of in front of countless,
This storm today night lives sad,
Thinking unlucky lacking my house,

That night cursed thoughts pricked me,
Found life childless wife with her dad,
Attending her sick father aged too,
Children in distant lands working,

Loneliness was killing felt remorse,
Even if rain troubling neighbors differ,
Family life warmth binds all close,
Dawn breaks and hoped sunshine,

Empty my home ghostly silent hunting,
Hunted not by fear but melancholy,
No children noise disturbances plenty,
The house would have to smile, electric,

God has graced whom I or neighbor,
Tears I felt welling up their life I prefer,

Let Lord give me poverty but family,
Enough children to crowd my bosom,

Willfully we would dance in the rain,
Sound with white noise raindrops,
Jubilant sighting of toads jumping,
Their horse noise is loud and scintillating,

Wiped tears, rolling, yes, Lord plays,
Give luxury, comfort, and wealth, yet deprived,
My wife is calling in the morning angry,
Demanded to be with her to assist,

Reluctantly I intimated the job, permit a little,
Working, no permission to leave office,
Cursed her life, helpless husband unfit,
Expressed her sad life father is sick,

Alone with her dad, tired, restless her life,
Smile a bit never replied to her strife,
Though she curses her fate, accusing,
Looked through the windows locality,

Innumerous houses families are living in,
Living alone widows husband no more,
Cursing Lord stealing her love cruelly,
Her heart urging for her husband crippled,
Even blind or deaf, crippled acceptable,
Twosome lives leading bestowed mumble,

Bewail Laborer

Never lament my soul console,
Fallen feathers hunt all whole,
Fragile limb writhing feel, fatigue,
Struggle live peril, win intrigue, (1)

Thwart humility, despise serve,
Break boundary wall hot nerve,
Incense painful wail move help,
Forget class, caste, creed, yelp, (2)

Assuages soothing words, belief,
Witness tortured spirit, in relief,
Timely, help save suffering sick,
Hate pretense alibis assist kick, (3)

Infinite satisfaction selfless test,
Life extends the day-night manifest,
Serve sufferers, weak, ill, cherish,
Water bubble burst trust perish, (4)

Infect smiles, sick recover adore,
Priceless gratitude n happy tears,
Unite family relived tension fade,
Kid gets father, mother back raid, (5)

Parents watch the child survives, smile,
Watch happiness tearful n while,
Erases past painful sight regain,
Selfless serves new vigor, me insane, (6)

Broken chain of notion, look life,
Keep behind, close window, strife,
Self-help motto best help, super,
Family, friends, and kin help superior, (7)

Born for faith community service,
Award reward, accolade call vice,
Born once unknown death steal,
Deathless spirit bold touch heal, (viii)

Seek death un-noticed unknown,
Conquer servitude, I die lovelorn,
Sojourn infinite memory lane lit,
All merciful guide energizes spirit, (9)

With each breath, feel His presence nit,
Amaze His image human face writ,
Service to suffering life serve God,
Learn ignorant mind, rest absurd, (10)

The transient realm invests illusive all,
Teenage to old age rhapsody recall,
Melody of desires manipulates nice,
Illiterate, I know humans pay the price, (11)

Sweet, sour human life, joy, agony,
Search for lifelong pleasure, company,
Sink wild mind celebrate to forget,
Scary past horror melt mist, relate, (12)

Hides mist reality mortal life short,
Dedicate my life, serve people, trust,
Squander life precious service save,
Contemplate cool, sit beside a grave, (13)

Peaceful Rest soul ah, walls absent,
Anger, hatred, greed, love, resentment,
False attachment allures light fade,
Bewail laborer n alerts, death evade. (14)

Bewildered Insight

Grew up in a temple town for pilgrims,
Converge from country, prayer extreme,
The deity in the temple has round eyes, no ears, palms,
No feet, round belly, red lips look calm,

As the child saw many cries aloud, tears on a roll,
Few laugh and whisper if Thanksgiving calls,
Visitors few focus on temple carvings exotic,
Many are busy savoring sweet ecstatic,

Buy idols, beads, fancy items, busy most,
Group squat in the courtyard, in gossip, lost,
There is a temple of a goddess, other, god,
Light oil lamps earthen, readily try to nod,

Few ordinary pilgrims sing a loud prayer,
Often dance in rhythm to onlooker share,
Saw aged people, women sitting quietly in the corner,
Reading sacred books eye, closing in prayer,

Beads silent roll long, curious seek ever,
Few hoist flags in the temple, pay for the charge,
Thousands of oiled wick burns crowd large,
Childhood left an imprint on memories,

Temple visits in innocent belief, glory,
Year-round celebration of festivals drag,
The millions of throngs, crowd marches with the flag,
Grew young, then adult Worshipped pure,

Never could know Lord listen, help assure,
Saw many a time lonely, before round eyes,
Learned visualizes our pain, desires in rising,
Ever insatiable greed, healings are met quick,

Trust and faith conviction or prayer do magic,
Ripe age, learned, the essence of divine grace,
Seekers ever surrender, practice, bless,
Legs and palms are invisible, deaf to listen,

Purity, righteous lives, rejection to listen,
Round eyes, all-knowing of deeds instant,
Whenever we commit, he sees from a distant,
As we sow, so we reap, good or evil mind,

Prayers, visits, and presence fails to remind us,
A plentitude of beggars, ill terminal, blind,
Deaf, partially able, mute, restitute, find,
Cheats, thieves, criminals, and killers mix well,

River of the soul a road a festival swell,
Perplex, cool-mind, Lord fixed looks silent,
Witness misdeeds, subtle, rarely prevent,
Never seen cure beggary, hunger, sick,

Limbs ever grew, disables right quick,
Woes of women abundant, ill-treated,
Molested in public, cruelly rejected,
Orphans host them to beg to converge,

Ever, the ocean of compassion did submerge,
Ever plight of destitute, women ill fate,
Infinite love, His grace, erases, reflects,
Ever His kindness saved victims stable,

Ever His wish heals sick, defects able,
Ever Lord punish cheat, criminals, fraud,
Ever Cruel, pretentious mind faces odd,
O Lord, in life, wicked tremble to death,

How come they visit the temple, donate wealth,
Gold, money, jewels heap as gift shower,
Ever they dread your mace to slaughter,
A time your gift amazes the human mind,

Weapon to obliterate the human race cleanly blind,
More virulent organic weapon mind create,
Spread like mind faster, invisible predate,
Silent tears warm roll, alone wet lips sip,

Bewildered insight, this mind does worship,
Life near the end could not fathom your rule,
So much violence, arson, cruel death, so cold,
Dictates, insight my heart, O Almighty,

Ever peaceful, happy my nation beauty,
Ever, women feel secure, children, their future,
Ever innocent, poor, destitute shelter,
Ever hunger dissolves, wellness growth,
Ever O almighty as warrior preserve worth,
Ever Lord decimate evil eternal definite,
Ever clear my bewildered insight?

Bewilders Voice

Listen instantly to a baby cry first,
Divine gift ear picks up, till last,
Human listens to voice noise swell,
Mind interpret meaning, all well,
Gradually baby learns to voice nice,
Astonish life a sound ever entice,
Heart aspire mind dreams choice,
Mystical intricate bewilders voice, (1)

Teenage life curious, sweet chirp,
Myriad bird sound pull sharp,
Wind changes speed to whisper,
Gentle breeze heart listens pure,
Shrill noises of wind and pass through leaves,
Raincloud roars thunder, heaves,
Flute organ instrument air plays,
Animal bird creatures create ways,
An infinite number of sound airwaves,
Bewilder voice let wilderness save, (2)

Mind is young to search a voice rapturously,
Murmur raindrops brook, rejoice,
Music instrumental plethora steals,
Mesmerizes the human mind, life feels,
Vibrations unknown, wave infinite,
Feeble gentle whistle audible excite,
Man animals and plant creatures enthrall,
Music is a realm that captivates moves regal,
Temple ring church bell usher bliss,
Cow-herd bell tinkle cuckoo call wish,
Music brings sleep and tranquility to enroll,
Music erases tension, fear, anger, all fall,
Musical nature life instrument rejoice,
Silence prevails, music bewilders voice, (3)

Eons, human life acknowledge a speech,
A treasure trove of millennium beseech,
Prophet, seer, monk, ancient script told,
Holy book sermons sanctified tell bold,
Human primitives communicate a symbol,
Immortal word coagulate spoken enroll,
Language spoken letter phenomenal all,
Human voice-encoded literature enthralls,
As much race equal spoken a language,
Human knowledge, tongues let privilege,
Beginning sound OM infinite dialect tail,
Communication enriches life send detail,
Human voice travels the globe with instant reach,
Bewilders voice world discussion bewitch, (4)

Recite ancient sage practice stored memory,
Transmit to next generation cross century,
Hindu holy script Vedas Vedantic Sanskrit,
Mythological details poems, prose interlink,
Travel time ocean recitation daily practice,
Ancient cultures discovered wisdom all exists,
Voice to memory reverse cycle faith rejoice,
Millennium pass, gurukul bewilders voice. (5)

(Note: Gurukul means ancient Vedic education abode,
Present Day University with one Rishi, Maharishi as a Teacher on all subjects of human knowledge.
The transmission was voice mode to recite n memorize.)

Bewitch Gesticulation

Exasperates, fail to communicate,
The heart longs for comradeship, intimate,
The lonely world tortures self, remorse,
Complacence search all, of course, (1)

Unknown person, a stranger to spirit,
Gradual intimacy gestures in discreet,
Strange river of life wider separate,
Separately at a glance indicates, (2)

Ink my emotion, love, earnest wish,
Sharing, pain, scars, agony establish,
Search lifelong a spirit trustworthy,
Able to confide humiliations, filthy, (3)

Life is less a bed of roses thorns wait,
Language of eyes, fingers, tell hate,
Tell O friend, a face how looks, abuse,
To bridge the river of life and confuse, (4)

Approach a few decent people, smile,
Sad, feel aloof some look way, style,
Ignore outright or gesticulate, rude,
Bridging friendship daunting crude, (5)

Decency, gentle heart, civilized spirit,
Smiles replies smile bridge discrete,
Intimacy grows faster gesture right,
Both friends we meet n faces bright, (6)

Speechless to pen, failing proper words,
Etches gesticulations, hands forward,
A hug, kiss, and pat I encounter visible,
Emotion happiness remorse simple, (7)

Bottled up for a long empty my heart,
Body entirely expresses language art,
I miss friends receive messages bit,
Gesticulation a language prick wit, (viii)

Ripe age find grandkid baby often
Life mingles with my love fascination,
Giggles baby, bewitch gesticulation,
Hard of hearing, mother, I converse,
Most easily gesticulates, of course, (9)

My life, my story, never limit gestures,
Eon humans communicate n secure,
The advent of language speech does exist,
Gesticulate primitive tribe we desist, (10)

Signs of limbs transmit quick symbols,
Witness traffic police vehicles roll,
Conclude memory of my college life,
Cement friendships later love strike, (11)

Nostalgic our communications best,
Never felt talking in a crowd intricate,
Messages of eyes essayed emotions,
Bewitch gesticulation stalk occasions, (12)

Gesticulation, I pray divine truly,
Never see my face plead Him, unruly,
Words fail to face, eyes express emotion,
Silent by heart, bewitch gesticulation.
Request watch the dance sequence lyrical,
Bewitch gesticulation surely enthrall. (13)

Bewitching Beauty

At the tender age of the school, encounter first,
Beauty is sweet to look at, enamors heart,
Lifelong time rolled slowly, rarely did fast,
Bewitching beauty hooked little to last,

The beauty of the female face never felt special,
Slip out of school, nearby beach enthrall,
Blue sea, surging waves incessant roar,
Golden sand dazzles cleanest to loiter,

Use to sit long hours watching birds,
Flying high in blue skies, never tired,
Fishermen sailing boat, mind afloat,
Distant coastal forest swings aloft,

The solitude, bright sunshine etch,
Bewitching-beauty in childhood stretch,
Grew younger passion for nature, beauty,
Heart missed, often bewitched slips duty,

Vast waters, placid coastal lake allure,
Boat sails, the wind gentle, birds much more,
The temple on a rock, in deity folklore,
The crowd loves a trip, beautiful lake, so sure,

Lost many a time in Greens, mountain,
On many occasions, heartthrob lo fountain,
Waterfalls, several rocks in color gleam,
Rainbows in summer-cool spirit clean,

Brooks in deep forest colorful tiny bird,
Creeping, soft, crawling at a bank, lizard,
Small fish in numbers steal look so long,
Rays of setting sun, forest in dusk song,

A trip by boat sailing in a river in life,
Village folk, goods from cities, smiles,
Goat, cycle, school kids, their laughter,
Bewitched in the beauty of innocence assure,

At night a journey by boat once on a full moon,
Overwhelmed by her charms, river own,
In silvery waters, alone with few silent,
Boat man's village song touching decent,

On tour, on duty traveled interior most,
Rural landscape imprinted spirit lost,
Green rice fields, swings enchant,
Bells of bullock cart attract, distant,

Cowherds, dust clouds, herdsman tall,
His long stick turban, loud call recall,
At a young age, lost in beauty n charms,
Village girl, colorful cloth, smile, and warm,

Kids playing on a village road, cycle tires,
Run along, in groups dances inspire,
Evening time village in darkness sleep,
Few oil wicks burn bright, village deity,

An aged man with Bhagavata, a bright lamp,
His narration, listen silent local rapt,
In the car, while return saw a kids crowd,
Curios eyes, noise, giggling a lot proud,

Left the village, dolls pitcher on the head,
Little child clinging cloth bare tread,
Glances as spark curious smiles,
Bathing ghat in pond prick miles,

Paradise on earth is my state, love,
Bewitching, her beauty, tears dissolve,
In, flights to big metros visit frequent,
Gleaming glass towers, flyovers went,

Luminescent cars speeding ahead,
Homes in concrete kissing sky red,
Huge parks, working place dazzle,
Huge colleges, hospitals, transit sizzle,

Million in the stream of life, evening light,
Shame dark night, music, club bright,
Saw beggars in the street, handsome men,
Youth with an attractive look, kids reign,

Scintillating in beautiful young women,
Colored designed dress, silk woven,
Few in ornaments, gold, jewels shine,
Admiring eyes, lips, smile, crisp lines,

Owed paradise on the moon, felt distant,
Forgotten in age busy life, reluctant,
Fading quick milling crowd, night sky,
A damsel in slumber lighted with a sigh,

Ripe age, mind traverse memory lane,
Natural beauty in my state, village women,
Purity, smiles, silence, solitude lure,
The smell of earth, mountain green allure,
In the lap of land, bewitching her beauty,
Sing her splendor, on earth executive.

Bird's Eye

A million stays in the middle top,
And days, hour wastage news hop,
Death clips live breed rumor incline,
In weeks infects, point faults prime, (1)

Like wolves, a few howls in cyberspace,
Fear, anger, hatred, cruelty neat lace,
Spread as a source curse own nation,
Ensure a doom get pleasure function, (2)

Let me live, noble leads and people die,
Beware, so thick skin bullet never fry,
So many places get support protection,
Instantly attack if preserve n defects, (3)

As a Trojan in the guise pretends innocent,
Kill, destroy, pollute secular decent,
A leader leads in wombs of destiny.
Decades got strong, smash mutiny, (4)

Defeat the face of this fate with a smile,
Death lurks in the guise in a mile,

Prayer of a billion the nation in love,
Unwell physical doctor medic resolve (5)

Infinite energy lead life, destiny, son,
Elected to assembly rule people run,
Elected to serve a massive look nation,
Destroy opposition n political blows,
Never people look who wins or owes, (6)

Silent in grave pandemic lament death,
The destiny of nation recovery wins health,
The game of discipline covers all states,
People of all ages listen to floodgates, (7)

Let a billion vaccinate earnest length,
Lord of the land protects our breath,
Lord protects not warriors but people,
A deadly virus fades in time as simple. (viii)
Every breath nurses awake toils hard,
Serve and love a people, ensure hope a reward,
Endless labor prayer least unanswered,
Be Allah, Lord Jesus, God graces much,
Again nation will shine happiness such, (9)

Came the year the country suffered gained immense,
The dear country, we stand firm with no pretense
We dream our land the paradise renews.
Fade corona memory hunt kids bemuse. (10)

Blind School

I came in contact with a child,
She is from a famous blind school,
Continuing her education funded,
Her school record was the best,
Performed, excellent in subjects,

Her encounter in the ancient temple,
Millennium old idols, still worshipped,
Throng pilgrims hundred thousand,
Center of culture ancient studies,
She was with a group of blind girls,

She was singing prayer eloquent,
The ancient language she was fluent in,
The first time heard such a sweet voice,
Aware of musical syntax breaks,
Flowed her charming voice electric,

The pilgrims noted, awed by her,
Disbelieve her memory of long poems,
Onlookers surrounded her, attentive,

Astonished the script mistake-free,
Clear recitations were distinct rightly,

Mesmerized loved melodious oration,
Stunned to notice her tears sparkle,
Her folded hands on her chest still,
Infinite her devotion prayer touched,
Approached her to the bus, introduced,

She smiled, happy I liked her prayer,
Humbly accepted praises and honestly,
Queried God's idol she could not see,
How she could feel devotion in tears,
Socked me, her reply Lord has seen her,

She knew the darkness in life managed,
The ancient script describes the Lord,
She could visualize to exact image,
Seven hundred lines she memorized,
Understood the poem belittled notions.

Blithesome Hours

Restricted to home watch time passing,
From dawn to dusk, leisurely life contemplates,
Night long lonely silently waits for morn,
Dreamless, past eventful life floats, touching,

The thrill, curiosity for the world, throbbing,
No more pulsating, the aging veins calm,
Desired capitulated long ago, discovery ended,
Enough cruelty, harsh world, jealousy, rivalry,

Bitter fights, revenge, false notions, quarrels,
War, destruction of nature, ruination, wanton,
Ruin pristine human character,
Generation gets frenzy, angry, frustrated,

Elusive peace, true happiness, love,
Loving humanity getting depleted, anguished,
Roamed countryside saw a crowded nation,
Amusement, physical pleasure, overwhelming,

No more desire to travel happily, confined,
Watch You-tubers hour after hour,
Time passes in the comfort of a sweet home,
That I built with lifelong savings, hard labor,

Modest pension, get care of wife,
Child, only son conscious of my health,
Feel caring, immense love of loved ones,
A cocoon, I found, expressive, only addiction,

I write my life that observed, perceived,
Praying Almighty knows dawn may not see,
Got education, success in life, wife, son,
Got respect in society, immense love too,

Simple life so peaceful, contented,
Awakened mind to inner consciousness,
Listen to whispers of the silence calmly,
Blithesome morning hours dawn breaking,

Another day, the graciousness of the Lord,
I shall live with pleasure, solace to my pen,
Watching blithesome hours is Praying,
Almighty, offering my soul, surrender.

Blood And Salt

Fascinate imagination, blood toil,
Hard work tames hazardous soil,
Arid, barren field rock-strewn nit,
Cultivate farmland strength and wit, (1)

Agrarian life ignores predicament,
Stubborn mind block derailment,
Segregates rock boulder manure,
Miraculous, strong-hand capture, (2)

Capture successful harvest raise,
Peasant endeavors, unique craze,
Vagary of weather vanquish mind,
Praiseworthy, accommodates find, (3)

Find a solution that sustains a population,
Feed, bountiful harvest promotion,
Sacred Land feeds, children nourish,
Drink river water her milk, flourish, (4)

Land satiates thirst, plants animals,
Her milk food creates blood, normal,

Minerals, inconspicuous add salt,
Her children built with muscle cult, (5)

People prosper with her gift of serene,
Harsh world, humans struggle n win,
Nature helpful grace profusion nit,
Bridal dress, the motherland explicit, (6)

Mountain her head hills are breast,
Flow her milk like a river feed crest,
Blood and salt strengthen iron fists,
Pull juggernaut rolls nation n wrist, (7)

Loud thunderous hail her supreme,
Save her sovereign, defend extreme,
Face voluntary, supreme-sacrifice
Mingle children's blood, salt suffice, (viii)

Accept salt, motherland in blood relief,
Faithful serve motherland spare life,
Patriotism wail myth service, dictate,
Leaders and scholars dedicated relate, (9)

Compensation is insignificant life free,
Share affluence joy gold care, agree,
Dismantle walls, break mistrust well
Fraternity bonhomie tolerance quell, (10)

Quell inequality discrimination total,
Radiate democratic rights n enthrall,
Corruption crimes surrender patriot,
Sacred-oath with constitution parrot, (11)

Clean life industrious strengthen nit,
Selfless, dedicated success, nail grit,
Civilization monumental well inspire,
Record human history neat transpire, (12)

Astonish people civilization has seen crumble,
Discovers blood salt in veins, grumbles,
Sacrifices for the motherland, vanity loot,
Treachery fuels greed, selfish act brut, (13)

Motherland in chain victorious enemy,
Blood n salt disappears, leaving the company.
Blood n salt revolts true children fight,
Battle cry thunderous might lead right, (14)

Sacred secrets destroy sacrilege in a jolt,
Decimate your own enemy alien, blood n salt,
Eon witness independence beacon again,
Flows blood n salt, mother graces vein. (15)

Blood Rose

Sensed the budding youth dreaming,
Love transforming to rose pink,
Sensation cold winds touched, fragrant,
Eyes were searching the source, busy,

Rain pouring drenched limbs enticed,
Mind ran like wild boar, never stopped,
Dissected wet earth, aromas sickening,
Acute desire modulated knew in vain,

The beauty of nature taunted, a brook murmured,
Butterfly flutters heart in a shudder,
Who, who are you stole me in dreams,
Heart stole, soul, lamenting in youth,

Saw a thousand smiles in posters pictures,
Jumped ever grab sight of a new smile,
Silent, unknown weaving spider net,
Felt heartthrobs, imagine acquaintance,

Saw in city streets, village fields adoringly,
A lightning spark vanished and struck spellbound,
Dark long hairs swaying, missed night sad,
Chrysanthemum these heart years after,

Lost the fragrance of many petals, the memories,
Failed a life to seek the adorable face, mate,
Stopped visiting these days in dreams,
Plucked the pink rose from this heart, unaware,

Pricked the thorn, blood as if dripping,
Socked there was no thorn in the heart,
Mind tricked life watching the blood rose,
Beautiful but a mirage that vanished for good,
Browning plant life wearing seek purpose,
Dews settle on petals, glaze smiles, blood rose.

Blue Planet

O' mind ever been in a deep forest and lost,
Greens all around, no path, meadows in front,
Ever slept in the grass, a flower bed, blue sky,
Mountains deep green all around, looking high,

Unreal silence, solitude yet pleasant, cool breeze,
Fragrances prevail all around from the flower trees,
Nearby plains, brook rapid on a rock, blue emerald,
Ever felt left to paradise human of the world,

Not fiction, a vision, six decades back in memories,
Seek in hungry heart, millions so, gone away in time,
Barren fields, rocky mountains, dry beds of rapid line,
Green cover, emerald blue, calm water, lotus, a lake,

The generation now, aliens of their own, mock all as fake,
Seven decades in the earth weathered seasons sad,
Warm summer, spring, and winter chill, a thrill onward,
The rain came, the monsoon break, people's indoor time,

Season of love, family bond, farmers in the field fine,
Fresh forests, swollen rivers, fairies play in fountains,
Mother nature ever in dress, flowers, ripe fruits shine,
Fragrances of wet earth, flowers, fruits, butterflies,

No more seen-gone oblivion species of our time,
Many did vanish, depleted animal life, hungry, thirsty,
Deserts, hot wind, storms plenty, nature got nasty,
Human greed, feasting in eyes, green forest loot,

If there is tomorrow, manifest horror, logs in wood,
Fed factories of paper, furniture, house goods,
The rest is forest land grab insane clear most in time,
Mines, cities, factories, infrastructure, so a crime,

The evening passed, late age in pain, seen as a curse,
The curse is for a new generation, lost if worse,
Never they saw the blue planet, enchanting beauty,
Nor will see, ever a time rolled back, rarest reality,

Air, water, forest cover, season change got worse,
Polluted air, toxic dust, and breathing are a curse,
Underground water, no more, fountains went dry,
Meadows and hills grass cover dried never let try,

Metropolis high-rise towers, metal roads, highways,
Concrete jungles replaced jungle rivers are a drain,
City sewerage, filth backyard, industries flush toxic,
Polythene earth, polythene river, oceanic surface thick,

In two decades, the world sees, the air will be hotter,
Underwater depletion further, all lack drinking pure,
Impure food is toxic a lot, health in the future is a dream,
A dead planet for water, air, food, toxic, return clean,

Inhospitable, barren terrain, dry bed of the river lake,
Hottest air, poisoned water, chemicals in food intake,
Melt my mind calmness gone upset in the heartfelt,
Late night in the dark balcony, lost in a thought quest,
Vanish world green emerald blue planet.

Boatman

The day I came to see this world,
Never knew strange crying aloud,
Learned smile later fun play a lot,
Sleep comes to a lot of time passes so quickly,

Days never guessed turned over a week,
A day in my life I got my dress,
Book and teacher, note, speak less,
In higher school, I saw never knew,

Who I am; rest on life to happen view,
So many faces laugh, the teacher stern,
Studying my parents so much concern,
New books smell, pen pencil notebook,

Dress boot ties passed left school look,
Came college in life gone technical,
New faces, new places, view magical,
My dreams, thoughts, and love went bright,

In time got service as study get completed,
Money in hand, the thrill in heart n pleasure,
Time ran fast, life changed, seeking treasure,
The family, home, and teenager,

I saw got married grew,
From dawn to dusk in my life, I only met a few,
Never know where all have gone far,
Alone in my home, sad, tears, despair,

Bondage, love, care, such chains in life,
A mid-day sleep after lunch, heavy n tight,
Saw a dream remember, incredible sight,
I like a boat was afloat alone in fright,

Nothing could I see near or far present,
Swirls of life like water were still at rest,
Calm waters under me watch lot swim,
Amazed as a boat watch lives, if all seem,

Memories hunt of my family world in love,
Water, of the life, expands far off, blue sky above,
Distant hills green in haze near the lake,
The sight fright my presence here as fake,

Dark one sitting end of boat, rowing or break,
He, in silence, guided me as a boat ashore,
Lost in thought as rowing speak in a whisper,
Nameless and no face you loved in life,

Forgot all time your home visit right,
All you passed as own, knew now unknown,
You sail the boat all along in utter illusion,
Feeling boat is only me, can't find the soar,

This picture is only metaphoric curious to trust,
Far of the hill your home to return must,
Your body you stay for lifelong now,
The spirit in your living is me to tow,

Ever call body as mine as this boat
Watch only you at the tip, other you thought,
Shed darkness to find you within,
Life is only an endless lake between,

Never knew all you passed as a fool,
Alone you are sailing here, differ to me!
Like a boat will be in anchor knows in time.
Got up in Jerk the boat n scene melts first,
Thought my time a day, reveal as last,
Calm mind, I plead silently in warm tears,
Boatman! With mercy, take me ashore...

The Body Is The Temple

The body is a temple,
Breathing is divine soul witnesses,
In ancient times, humans knew the creator,
Lives spent in solitude, caves, forest cover,

Sat for decades no water food but a breath,
Bare the body weather season seek at length,
Heavy rain, hottest days, the cold season saw,
Amazingly human, modern times, a fact yet bow,

Indomitable spirits seek even this time a lot,
Never treat self-publicity secret of life all got,
Only know the truth divine to seek not out,
Deep within Divine dwell all breath subtle,

Years passed, seek the soul, search the invisible,
Inner is darkness, glistening nothing, proceed slowly,
Intuition awareness calm mind breath low,
Mind slow, thoughtless, result vision clear,

Intelligence pursue within wisdom so near,
Every human being do have divine within,
The body is a temple no one searches win,
Life is busy, so the enchanting mind is the twin,

Latter led to life external in thought getting lost,
Life passes own time till quitting the most,
Few Minds inspire strong forsake lure,
Reject all pleasure lust possession assure,

Leave community keep solitude in a quest,
Own resolve pain suffering ever face test,
No easy path, most complicated, lonely,
A time comes the divine shines brightest only,

Deep within inner vision dispels the dark,
The soul within witnesses all merges a spark,
The human goes lifeless, breathless no pulse,
Divine grace awakes the soul slow on impulse,

Consciously awake, impart wisdom, realizes the truth,
Defeat death stays subtle and appears at will the fruit,
Seer is capable, perceives divine presence,
Million in his path far from civilization affluence,

Lonely devoid of family asset river confluence,
Deep forest mountain caves defeat influence,
Human shows why to waste precious life presence,
Luxury comfort family bond assets eminence,

Disease, hunger, fear, horror, inhuman existence,
Love, compassion, surrender, natural ambiance,
Knew own soul once departed, liberated in silence,
Aspired long soul get back own home in space,

Return on divine will but enlightened n blessed,
Divine Will, all accomplished, never again come,
The alien world, beast do feast rest welcome,
The ignorance covers every sojourn of the soul's curses,
Fail to break, birth n death, a chain, pain, sadness,
The body is the temple,
Breathing is divine, soul witness.

Bolster Epitome

Quiet metropolis twilight encroach,
Smokes raise cloud lives approach,
Intoxicate aromas suburb sight nit,
Laborers return late families greet, (1)

Spider nets narrow paths gleam-lit,
Happiness resides here joy, discreet,
Incredible life, mysterious, smiles all,
Dirty faces invite glinting eyes to enthrall, (2)

Small kids play trivial studies often,
Lotus from muddy pond rise notion,
Talent, courage, aspirations hidden,
Tiny-seed sprouts giant tree, smitten, (3)

Inherits castes lower curse well bite,
Poor working-class labor despite,
Blemish acquires nil struggles hard,
Cruel fate by birth wins less reward, (4)

Money, meager income deprive child,
Education needs money results to yield,
Scholarship offers state people to strive,
Education, game, sport, and youth thrive, (5)

Free country ignore, color class faith,
Skill n performance treasures wealth,
Roots get nameless face obscure soul,
Trailblazer performances zenith goal, (6)

Career scales adhere to an executive post,
Achieves leadership visionary almost,
Inspires nation least forget root clear,
Glorious life inspires land, remember, (7)

Simple life, few clothes, less asset gold,
Single soul inspires people best mold,
Clean life disciplines strong, decisions,
Leads nation single-handed devotions,(viii)

Selfless service demeanors commoner,
Billion-plus people elect the same winner,
Youths children learn lessons, dismay,
Where there is will there exist the way, (9)

Slum dweller leads billion of people neat,
Astonishes rich, powerful, feel discreet,
Never unique case nations witness all,
Lotus grows from muddy water, recall, (10)

Hardship struggle endurance, courage,
Qualities extraordinary person craze,
Power corrupts absolute power totally,
Gold, fame, applause corrupt ego tally, (11)

Unparallel spirit never influences ego,
Slum-dwellers, charismatic, smile agog,
Decimates deprivation discrimination,
National unity bolsters, strongly caution, (12)

Selfless service to people nation grows,
Peace, progress, essential dictate vows,
I once walk, evening darkens slum gully,
Electric-feeling spread darkness wooly, (13)

Aromas intoxicate laughter permeates,
Human smile n depravity reciprocates,
Stays standstill in the dark, contemplates,
Motherland needs poor kids to dominate. (14)

Bone Of Contention

Mischievous-heart seeks neat pleasure,
Search paradise luxurious life treasure,
Mischief gold cloth food create, enamor,
Mind captures body enjoys egos clamor, (1)

Story-begins human love, power, glamour,
Believes body-is-life satisfaction is secure,
Fate, little open gate of fortune intimate,
Seed of own action sprout communicate, (2)

Good deeds bring fare-result harvest nit,
Bountiful Earth provides hard work greet,
In time plow soil, work, row seedy plants,
Harvest in time come seasons supplant, (3)

Green corn field ripe to lustrous golden,
Human nature, watch time strictly even,
Opportunity rarely visit revisit not again,
Make late once run lifelong finds in vain, (4)

Driving mind alert initiates effort, control,
Lacunas negate, lacks lethargy, fetch goal,
Wiser spirit simple peasant knows notice,
Generations inherit, experiences, practice, (5)

Ah, look the urban life will search for leisure,
Several-way games betting mint pleasure
Easy life, easy money multiply quickly all,
Hit jackpot chit-fund provides n enthrall, (6)

Money asset goes away to lose everything,
Rich faces the fate of rags, curses, luck vetting,
Focus spirit, inner ego wrought havoc nit,
Leisure comfort without work demand bit, (7)

Blames ill fate, ill luck, missed fortune related,
Furious state display quickly as time dictates,
Reject funny discipline control rules time,
Begs another chance for money on loan fine, (viii)

Inks canvas, not fiction reality permeate,
Every sphere of life, across ages, create,
Literate, intelligent, wiser, knowledgeable,
Commits blunder, reject outright, trouble, (9)

Alone exhibits tension, anger, fear, sorrow,
Paradoxical, the same life asks for tomorrow,
Long-life witnesses often family ruins nit,
Innocent children find no future discreetly, (10)

Human nature extends issues, indefinite,
Bitter arguments tread discussions fight,
Betting prospers vetting wiser cheating all,
Money spinning machine rolls right-stroll, (11)

Watch long arms of the law n mute spectators,
A machine earns money, a human loses an actor,
Money n money sweeter than honey sings,
Trees give fruit, little bears money, brings, (12)

Human nature acts timely elephant walk,
In an idle mind, a pack of dogs barking,
Elephant; that looks behind not elephant,
The dog that never barks, not dog instant, (13)

Truth is truth alters again, truth in motion,
Accept or reject stand, bone of contention.
Controversy never ends, dust-storm gather,
Discussion clip progress, compromise never. (14)

Bonhomie

Great nation a billion people own,
Fascination imaginative, shown,
A myriad of ecstatic moments say,
Incredible achievements displayed, (1)

Courage love confluence exhibit,
Distrust, suspicions, hurt, prohibited,
Fight bitter casteism faiths hide,
Vows, dismantle walls n preside, (2)

A great effort to remove illiteracy,
Educations add skill supremacy.
Violence, riot, protest, big news,
Demands leaders discuss huge, (3)

Quells anger, solutions discover,
Implements laws fast do ensure,
Education excels in multifold fields,
Peace progress hit targets yield, (4)

Shield secure frontier alert well,
Bravery supreme sacrifice dwells,
Industry agriculture exceeds lot,
Peace satisfaction perform effort, (5)

Discover, innovate, force multiply,
International recognition qualifies,
Import, export trade secure gold,
Qualities the best promoter bold, (6)

Defense space explorations neat,
Adventure, a nation shines meet,
Alluvial landscape desert icecap,
Surrounds ocean mountain gap, (7)

The great rivers, fertile soil influence,
Eon civilizations establish sense,
Widest-culture, rich ancient exist,
Numerous language lifestyle list, (viii)

Century, under alien occupation,
Invaders, colonial rules in motion,
Century brings slavery massacre,
Ancient monuments ruined pure, (9)

Miss people in chains sufferance,
Unity, struggles, freedom, chance,
Dedicate life sacrifice clean, serve,
National duty selfless all deserve, (10)

Independence August arrive well,
New vigor inspirations past quell,
Future Hope celebrates the brightest,
Immense belief and trusts invest, (11)

Unite billion-plus hearts projects,
Bitter fights, doubt, anger rejects,
Good news Olympic result award,
Gold, silver, bronze, huge reward, (12)

News spread gold medal enjoy all,
Frenzy hilarious entire nation call,
Hype media daylong elaborate nit,
Great bonhomie visible light spirit, (13)

Across all sections of age n gender,
All class caste color merges sheer,
Dance sweet distribution match nit,
Bonhomie-visible extraordinary, lit. (14)

Book

Cradle of civilized humans preserved on life,
A billion aspects in a fascinating world thrive,
Often human eyes, ears, and skin fail detection,
All have a limit beyond stretches the realm,

Humans treat everything never notice a bit,
Ignorant mind tags all puzzles it fails, all wit,
Rare a perceptive mind focus on a phenomenon,
Analysis logic convolute to a concrete decision,

Theories reveal glorious most enlighten ignorantly,
Book is a multitude of types of palm leaves ancient,
Wall paintings rock in scripted times' variants,
Paper of centuries-old books enriches knowledge,

Million issues transformed in time scale in phase,
All recorded prying eyes search aware of the truth,
Awareness of each subject reveals a path to fruit,
Awareness churn the mind, and thought concept get clear,

An attitude of mind trusts vision examine point sheer,
Innovation involutes the focal point of imagination as a tool,
Books are thousands in number, imprint all as, rule,
Time saw most rules were proven wrong later,

Imagination float blocks it, turn myopic color,
Knowledge is the light path of life, enlightens brighter,
Chain of the unknown, all in-dark opposes freedom,
Knowledge breaks the chain, live enjoying freedom,

Freedom-of-the human mind triggers motion a lot,
Information concept attitude imagination alert,
All mobile positive thinking brings a new age,
The book changes its home library to the digital stage,

The world has seen floppy, disk drives, tape magnetic,
Further mutants hard drive pen drive majestic,
Millennium saw books transformed into information,
In an age enacted books fly on the internet, in digital form,

The world has gone ahead to cyberspace host books,
A billion books miniaturized atomic space hook,
All are within reach of the general man in search,
Instant takes time book reaches for research,

Book in the latest avatar signifies human freedom,
Freedom and natural human values are now in blossom,
O' book a heart in gratitude from teen to old one,
As breath, you accompany humanity hated by one,

Comics, stories literature information are classic,
The modern age imposes study books minimum of a basic,
The book got birth from a memory of the human mind,
For thousands of years, generations stored only this kind,

The name of the book in ancient India is Smriti n Shruti,
One memorizes in a lifetime narrates pupils to learn,
No book in a paper a teen recites on and on,
Then, turn into a career in the books studied in Ashram.

Book life transcends from space to space encrypted,
Subtle in its size and shape, future stored all in the void,
His angelic touch of the book sparks freedom of mind,
Who seek book pours light neighed love but find,
Book is the secret path humans move on realization,
Once the bondage of birth gets broken spirit never returns.

Bourgeois Mind

History eons reveal endless the struggle,
Innocent life suffers painfully wriggle,
Exploit, brute power, merciless rule,
Unknown courage revive, wonderful, (1)

Face certain-death dungeon lament,
Sacrifices life willfully fiery n nascent,
Passionate about equal rights, freedom,
Right to live decently, ask for free opinions, (2)

Demands to dismantle class n creed,
Hatred discrimination colludes breed,
Highlights stigma profess enigma lit,
Bright-future deserved winner is grit, (3)

Voluntary sacrifice n selfless motive,
Unites mass struggle words emotive,
Lives in prison dark chambers write,
Passion for freedom fuel struggle grit, (4)

Sneak, out of wall stronghold strong,
Inflames docile people, words if, song,
Inspires every word, a sharper sword,
Annihilate slavery, poverty fires word, (5)

Just n rightful born free breaks wall,
Magic wand light poems dare squall,
Recite child, youth, adult, old vocal,
Pervade script by heart phenomenal, (6)

Scripts recite famine epidemic horror,
Wipes out people, macabre sight fear,
Empty, silent village barren corn-field,
Savage human greed reign lives yield, (7)

Cower, desires to live, subjugate brute,
Dark-history slavery rebellion tribute,
Song invites people-in-chain eloquent,
Rise O' skeletons break chain n fluent, (viii)

Crush fortress of prison grumble fight,
Emancipation, birthright, dawn delight,
Bourgeois mind decent gift rare, think,
Dark dungeon chamber creates n ink, (9)

Vogue notions initially appear in a torrent,
Bourgeois mind mightier neat coherent,
Mightier is a pen than a sword, defeats exploit,
Exploiter bites dust Independence belt, (10)

Bourgeois class decent discipline adore,
Builder of nation doctor engineer allure,
Progress ensures research n education,
Middle-class people majority in motion, (11)

Pleader, leader, farmer rises on a ladder,
Visionary in jail, equally-free open folder,
Leads the world of media to think tanks to pen,
Forecast future clearly tame dogma chain, (12)

Blare clarion call alert exposes corrupt,
People are aware of bourgeois mind disruption,
Cleanses social fabric secure prosperity,
The spinal cord of the nation exhibits maturity. (13)

Hats off to the nurse, driver, soldier, worker,
Salute to, teacher, miner, official, writer,
Night of slavery captive end dawn break,
The bourgeois mind enchants a serfdom wreck. (14)

Broken Bridge

Intimacy once happened life, intrinsic,
Stimulated energy opulent happiness,
Forgotten feet upon ground ai the air,
Jumping spirit yet shouted at nothing,

Vacantly voiced overjoyed heart freely,
Worth living an insignificant life, lucky,
Every second preoccupied mind sense,
Let not the relationship melt into the air,

Clasped her hand, promised everything,
Middle-class youth educated dreamed,
Dare to dream angelic face disbelieved,
Study success and career enabled today,

Changed unpolished dirt clothes a few,
Dress immaculately, polished differently,
The unruffled dark oily hair, shy face,
Fumbled speaking confidently, remember,

How time-motivated metamorphoses,
Fluency in his utterance, suave and gentle,

Sparkles in his dark eyes were his past,
Still glinting with smiles attractive,

The voice, soft and soothing, introduced,
Talking to his girlfriend confidently,
Secured life plum post salary solvent,
Enough to trap the heart of a young female,

The introduction then discussions,
The thickening friendship's gradual bond,
Engrossed in a talk at restaurants, parks,
The pair in love are seen over the city,

At odd hours on the lonely riverfront,
The girl with an appeasing dress, fragrant,
Trying her best to match the youth,
She gets acquainted with him, informed,

His name village parents status well,
Conveyed her details equally by now,
The bridge has been erected, fascinating,
Growing strong by meeting every odd hour,

A call is ringing at odd hours continuous,
Calls lasting for hours seem never-end,
Growing intimacy families aware of,
The pair now visiting places enjoying,

The bridge is emboldened by trust,
Well understanding each other, nature,
Aware of habits, passion, each harbor,
It has been weeks past a few months,

All of a sudden surprised young man,
His girlfriend proposed marriage soon,
He was happy and agreed to marry,
Alas, the climax collapsed before it started,

The female got foreign service prestigious,
Her family blocked decided to date, time,
Her father got adamant and canceled,
The future of the daughter is visible,

Should not surrender her life, a housewife,
Future prosperity both guaranteed,
Missing girlfriend these days, sadly,
The youth contacted her and said goodbye,

Astonished and she disbelieved,
She is rejected by him, happy,
Socked to see the broken bridge,
Collapsed from both sides, lost pillars,

She came to know about his migration,
Foreign job classy life than family life,
Equally strolled her long future,
He wished her excellent career status,

Speechless, the female in a sock,
Started probing the broken bridge,
Equally aspirant selfish heart spare,
Contemplating her soul and how to share!

Buoyant Spirit

Curious if you are crying under a veil,
Crushed your dreams, confined life,
Hurt over centuries of evil practice,
Freedom denied for your liberty, travel,

Freedom; education restricted,
Debarred mixing with men in society,
Guide men for walking in the open,
Early marriage, death at delivery of a child,

Widowhood curse for living treated as evil,
Snatching bangles, vermilion dots,
Banned long black hair, white cloth,
A separate room life imprisoned till death,

Read motherhood in restrictions in customs,
Generation women faced humiliation,
Deprived of the right to cremate her father,
Debarred rights denied by temples to touch idols,

Segregated, inequality, burning issues,
Reformed banned wife burning live if widows,
Banned child marriage, girls going to school,
Coeducation, inter-caste marriage reality,

A widow can remarry, settle in life if desired,
Leading prestige position, no dark spot,
Happened Independence liberty is a birthright,
More women educated lead society,

Equality liberty for girl child veil faded,
Celebrity, modeling, actor in cine-world,
A household name, eyes, lips, got contest,
The youth ran for female actors, famous rich,

Advanced nation after independence,
Women entered to armed forces and military,
Running corporate, industry, finance,
Leader of nation supreme authority,

Enigma shines personality, knowledge,
No darker chamber, past horror,
Dictating now my country govern,
Might of the female power no showpiece,

Cementing bricks of the nation strong,
Guiding research, technology, treating sick,
Assets of the country in sports win gold,
Nightmarish childbirth mortality little,

Marriage after education is preferred,
Transformation, glorious future, symbol,
Women holding the key to a nation,
Smiling, fear nonexistent opine,

Criticism, condemnations, lauded praises,
Buoyant spirit of women never before,
Deserving occupying the highest office,
Pillar of the constitution chief of Defense,

Respect obliged nation reverently,
Happy motherland flutters tricolor,
Happy mothers, children caring, respect,
Happy girl child grabs gold in every field,

A happy young woman leads the army in pared,
Happy women head of corporate, ruler,
The buoyant spirit presidential palace,
True freedom equality tricolor flutters.

Butterfly Sketch

Night progress, tired limbs freeze,
Alert mind sterile sleep in, breeze,
Sunken swollen desire disappears,
Silence creeps mind, dream near, (1)

Bed lamp glimmer in faint darkness,
Windows hide landscape redress,
Distant lamp posts draw solitude,
Empty road, dark home multitude, (2)

Bright my world amiss transforms,
Disintegrates human noise forms,
Violence, anger quarrels none exist,
Boundaries wall we erect fade list, (3)

Darkness-of-night crumples cover,
Speed dark earth in cosmos ether,
Appear star-studded sky, moon-lit,
Gleam forest hills field silver light, (4)

Surreal sight light shadow play nit,
Agonies hide, love desires delight,
Sun hides total, mid-night weaves,
Weave dream fantasy null grieves, (5)

Wild grass dances in winds, gentle,
Purple lavender, pink flower mettle,
Covers subconscious tension, pain,
Amazes dream world joyful remain, (6)

Butterfly sketch magic spell, reveal,
The scar of my past event quickly heal,
Steal name, face, identity address,
My soul in freedom forget distress, (7)

Free from dungeon butterfly image,
Colorful wings among flower mazes,
Incredible the realm change canvas,
Beautiful hill brook miss a morass, (viii)

Rainbows the spring clouds sketch,
Immortality of ambrosia forest etch,
No fear, death, fever, or hunger stalk,
No crowd, angel fly white fairy walk, (9)

Sweet music pervades omnipresent,
Fruit garden beautiful home decent,
Soul inhales aromas of ripe fruits wild,
Curios to the house enter wills yield, (10)

Empty home bed clean tidy is cover,
Glisten furniture, shine floor and mirror,
Butterfly watch on mirror image miss,
Realize soul dream unreal only bliss, (11)

Rests mortal frame inert forgets total,
Nice, butterfly sketch dreams enthrall,
Offer bliss plenty of bountiful quiet hours,
Soul desperate to feel limbs with the power, (12)

Dawn breaks elusive world entices lit,
Golden rays melt, mist discover great,
Dream-world fades, quick to sunlight,
A mystery, a dual entity, stays day-night, (13)

Pain, pleasure, love, hatred, anger hike,
Petals of lotus rose to differ like-dislike,
Butterfly betray happy a nightly sojourn,
Keep colorful wings, sketch nicely, morn. (14)

Cactus Blooms

Thousand cactus anger bloom,
Desperate soul in the darkest moon,
Empty womb of fertile soil cry,
Child withers sooner cruel fry, (1)

Dark smoke spreads, suffocate,
Breathless spirit dying dictate,
Flee hasty soul soil burns fail,
Barren mountain cavern trail, (2)

Horror points death savor tall,
Black raven top meet hit skull,
Flutters devil message threats,
Surrender survives, it recreates, (3)

Subjugate people chains tight,
Force kidnap youth knife fight,
Booms gunpowder all thunder,
Country-men remind blunder, (4)

Forget to kill the snake, ignore feel,
Fangs spread countrywide kill,
Lack monster love heart softer,
Search for blood kingdom lure, (5)

Kingdom of evil promulgate fly,
Condemn own soil clam, purify,
The Ocean of life split wide in tides,
Swirling river of life wish hides, (6)

Tsunami, of macabre sights, tell,
Search over the globe exists hell,
Mute deaf wise learned faithful,
Consoles world over reasonable, (7)

Portray colors of liberation bold,
Support wash sins purify, blood,
Calm witness amuse holocaust,
Neighborhood burns evils boast, (viii)

Globe runaway skies sketch nit,
Flights happen never before hit,
Escape from death-valley faster,
Take freedom-loving nit secure, (9)

Hectic actions war-footing etch,
Relief security future all sketch,
Unstable nation die cactus grows,
Bloom melancholy, scents owes, (10)

Terror won homeland establish,
Happy neighbor boasts feverish,
Age of salvations cactus brings,
Desert blooms skull head sings, (11)

Unseen almighty ashamed hide,
An ocean of tear submerges, deride,
Perplex cold heart globe portrays,
Cower at black menaces dismay, (12)

Mass exodus changes nameless,
Lost sacred soil alien if distress,
Bottle up loud sobs, smile mask,
Little favor from Lord bends ask, (13)

Sacred-land of almighty betrays,
Repentance kill-serpents delays,
Burn bamboo flute never sings,
Ignorance let, devil grows stings, (14)

The devil in the heart and seeks mercy,
Kindness and love turn poison fishy.
Cactus blooms turn time-wheel,
Repent most evil notion fate seal. (15)

Capitulate Life

A rose so pinkly, enwrapped in memories,
Teenage, I used to pluck in a park,
Loved much tiny heart, dreams rosy.
Innumerable sweet nights trip in a valley,

Thousands of roses color rainbow spray,
Use to lose myself, heartbroken at dawn,
Remember School, offer roses, a habit,
Friend teachers alike smile instantly,

Adolescence in hues rose, so romantic,
Loved felt shy offering roses to girlfriends,
Taunts teasing me ran from the company,
Lost in books etched in a study room,

World in revelation, glue to books,
The beginning of a phase rose fade,
Dream aspiration entwine heart heavy,
The night dream weaving valley,

Wanderlust, dream mirages, thirst,
Career rosy, expectations at the zenith,
Minor lack of luxuries for calmness,
Time on a wheel rolled fast, missed the rose,

Farewell with roses, tears to swell,
Back to my life, fragrances intoxicate,
Memory nostalgic sweep past me,
Sat lonely look at a rose, my teenage love,

Eyes in weight closing heard a whisper,
O' spirit, the wanting sutures sadness,
Childhood and smiles divine innocence,
The fragrance epitome of existence,

Time is to search within at home,
Early dawn, sat in silence calmly,
Within a rose, lose identity, time stood,
Hours passed, conscious, listening to,

See yourself now to exist an awareness!
O' spirit high up at great heights,
Focused seek your home in a void,
Experiences a dark sky stars mysteries,

The inner vision is thoughtless, limitless,
A blue light in the center, a rose shines,
Experience a blissful state, found my home,
Alien here all so beautiful reel life,

Came out of the union to light and smile,
Call to my heart inner world, what a sight!
The rose rules in inner consciousness,
The rose enraptures imaginations limitless,

Amazing one casts a rose,
A metamorphosis of life,
Sojourn with a great message,
In the universe prevails forever....

Cardinal Credence

Self-awareness blooms intimate,
Teenage enchant curiosity late,
Day unfold automatic progress,
World awake busy-life, impress,(1)

Events happen in time, miracles,
Dawn to dusk in orders, simple,
Morn call bird delights freedom,
Blue-sky bird circle lo abandon, (2)

Evening witness bird seek nest,
Humanity, tiresome search rest,
Incredible dreamland manifest,
Night thickens, canopy, dark test, (3)

Noisy-world arguments conflict,
Anxiety aspersions scorn, inflict,
Hurt heart acid tongue complex,
Lies guise pretentious lives vex, (4)

Anger smolders the mind to act violently,
Conscience goad soul be decent,
A bright sunny day entices the mind,
Conspire to revolt, rebels unkind, (5)

Influence teenage mind corrupt,
Evening prayer silences abruptly,
Peace n a calm mind, divine ensure,
Reason focus error warn future, (6)

Unknown, unseen divine, if talk,
Mind reading a sacred book, walking,
Book details His presence clear,
A big tree in seeds dreams future, (7)

Tiny-seed contain contour tree,
In time His wish translates to being free,
Air un-born wind travel endlessly,
Obey divine order breaths bless, (viii)

Rain collects water travels often,
Ocean obeys order share motion,
Raindrop nectar of life seed grow,
In-time in-command foliage glow, (9)

Feel His presence blossom smile,
In-time fruit ripens attached a while,
Seed travels worldwide, His mercy,
Landscape forest covers courtesy, (10)

The season follows in order, discipline,
Animals eat grass, and flesh live clean,
Never betray nature to safeguard,
Species send a message, forward, (11)

Read the book further truth, trust lit,
Conscience n intuition, a divine gift,
Attachment temptation duet sing,
The death-knell of human in end ring, (12)

The mind gets blind, lead, paths fence,
Conjure miracles betray credence,
Evening prayer over, I contemplate,
Surprised humans doubt Lord or hate? (13)

Precious life, Lord says, be humble,
Lead a life pure, trust the truth, simple,
Worship, love, care, serve Earth nit,
Preserve nature His image explicit, (14)

Regularly irregularly ignore a prayer,
Irregularly regular lo dream desire,
Indeed human deeds pay due results,
Mango tree ever give fruit cocoanut! (15)

Tearfully prayers, Lord, give me the patience,
Conjure trap, vow cardinal credence.
Greatest enemy, spirit doubt intense,
Betrays very birth, end in confluence. (16)

Catastrophe

Civilization is glorious, human creativity in ages,
The globe with monuments incredible,
Time passed thousand years engraved in rock,
Lost civilizations came to light pasts in shock,

Konark statues are alive and world overlooked,
The great art in Taj, other sites, time overtook,
Knowledge human perceptions realization enact,
Crystals strewn over the land, ocean,

Millennium, the twentieth century, glisten,
Humans broke the frontier of the unknown,
Mountains, plains, skies, depths of an ocean,
Broke the wall of suffering, illness, hunger,

Across nations, ages, races, and tropical places,
Final frontier deep space, in remote voyages,
The expanse of phenomena dimensions in light,
Space odyssey settling in distant planets,

Knew as mortals, built inroads for the future,
Human survival, inhospitable nature, to exist,
A new millennium broke the hope and aspirations,
Took shape into blazing crystals precious,

From dust they raised, in dust, they rest in cycles,
Earth, water, fire, air, space cohesion to life,
The human mind to conceive frontiers of spirit,
When arrive time to quit is unknown to the mind,

Failed to breach the domain of souls,
Millions of concepts of theories, unseen,
Deathless, no shape or size, nothing,
Feelings none, aspirations none, tests none,

Descend, get identities chain in a dual world,
Run after the mirage of lust n dreams,
The concept of indestructible, invincible,
Nature taught many occasions ravages,

Tidal waves, cyclones, earthquakes, forest fires,
Millions perished in the wave-rebuilt spirit,
Came to a microbe, muted so virulent,
In death, it spread into life spread saw the time,

Seen as a bolt from the blue, a race shaky,
Metropolis turned lonely cities lockdown,
Crystals crumbled if own deeds to disaster,
Cohesions of elements to vibrant life, splitting,

in months the unseen predator lesson to humans,
A catastrophe to eliminate than nature unwinding,
The heat, rain, wind, flood, and air are so toxic,
Nothing could convince humans of horrific,

So subatomic, conspicuous a microbe catastrophic,
From greed and false glory to a simple life nature friendly,
Not a predator, humans get cured of metamorphic,
Collapsing cohesion and conspicuous catastrophe.

Charisma

Feminine beauty charisma influences,
Enamor the human mind in luminescence,
Dark hair glistens, waves entrap quick,
Gorgeous embroideries silk sari click,

Eyebrows and dark lines catch sight nicely,
Deer eyes sparkle, glances mesmerize,
Gentle straight nose, milk complexion,
The face resembles a full moon in Redemption,

Lips are the invitation to enslave pride,
Soft arms, long, enticing, embracing, and tight,
A soul meek within arms tight in prison,
Loses cool, mind resisting loss is the reason,

Ornaments, necklace in gold is bright,
Charisma reflects heaven's angel delight,
Whispers none, charisma, looks allure,
Captivates thousand of souls total galore,

Charisma loves powerful dictates a blind,
People honor in life the wrong deed never find,
Charisma shelters with mighty and brutal,
The mind of human speechless surrenders totally,

Charisma befriends courage, daredevil,
Impacts the mind of a viewer, rewards in the anvil,
Turns charisma hostess for art, craft, music,
Excellent creations in time hunt nostalgic,

Charisma loves the poor, rich with golden hearts,
Serving people in crisis rescues life fast,
Charisma visits caring hearts for sick,
Lightens souls fight, saving lives at risk,

Charisma gets entangled with innovation,
Sweeps a time in a blitz with transformation,
Charisma gets captivated by a marvelous mind,
Enraptures the mind of a visitor to investigate to find,

Charisma shares glow in myths n valor,
People in generations read stories to savor,
Charisma matchless beauty unseen ever,
Her presence with spirit influences enamor,

A people in turmoil with violence, hopeless minds,
Charisma embalms painful body to rewind,
Charisma tests the detached mind in seduction,
A seeker resists glamour, corroding delusion,

Emancipation wins, charisma surrenders last,
The enlightened mind of seer dawns on realization fast,
Voice, advice, guidance for ignorant in the globe,
Fragrances of charisma intoxicate, ego disrobe,

Purity, the truth of life, rejection in birth and death,
Charisma, an angel convinces prayer is wealth,
A million souls surrender their hearts in prayer, often,
Charisma brings tears to wounded hearts in lotion,

Charisma never a mortal amazing in love,
Freedom of life, mind, faith, a vision evolve,
Charisma is elegance for the soul of humans,
Charismatic personality exists enemy no one.

City Life

Hypnotizes rural home

Tell tasteless saga, life rustic,
Born amid verdant hill music,
Enthrall childhood, call a forest,
Recline on rock eyes lost rest,
Steals crystal-clear brook lot,
On pebbles, it murmurs most,
Colorful bird strange whisper,
Gentle breeze leaves shudder,
Silent valley aroma wildflower,
Seclusion creates a love to shower,
Small village community close,
Parent, uncle, brother, sis owes,
Time-tested tranquil verdure,
Quit when young miss nature, (1)

Awestruck adopt life in the city

Blind city-light dazzles traffic owes,
Tall skyscrapers, avenues, live shows,
Milling mall is a busy bazaar and park,

Cement road clean lot of cars park,
Heart amazed, university, college,
Big office building or knowledge,
Neatly dress n school kids fluent,
City on the first visit all sink affluent,
Amazes mostly, wealthy and wise,
Nestled in a village hut in surprise,
Speechless fearful in sock begins,
College and university degrees win,
Luck job promotes a better life,
Nestle in city life with a kid wife, (2)

Opulent life city offered

Forgot mud cottage a sweet home,
House on brick cement mansion,
Small garden, two floors of windows,
Balcony nice asset furniture owes,
Due course, cars in the garage n bikes,
Life prospers in years desire hikes,
Food cloth travel ornament family,
Never conceived to happen so simply,
Bank balance life insured in the craze,
Opulent lifestyle luxuries purchased,
Air-condition television, all gadgets,
Conceivable pleasure all confiscates,
Life accrues luxury comfort in strife,
Miss peace recluse nestle in city life (3)

Sick in the city chose village home

A sleepless night in cushion tension,
Worries fetch illness diet is a reason,
Oil, spices, rich food tastily savor,
Tour late-night workloads harbor,
Pollution noise adds to health worsen,
Wish to quit the job and return to my village own,
Recall fresh air, peace of mind, joy,
Tranquil fields in greeneries enjoy,
Crowd, noise, dust, busiest life, miss,
Enamor rustic teenage, again kiss,
Time never revisits the past start again,
Nestles in city life, desires in vain,
Call of a village not audible in strife,
Village enamors end nestles in city life. (4)

Clay Idol

Infinitesimal scrutiny baffles,
Admiration, adulation ruffles.
Infinite beauty attraction well,
Caught sight of damsel, swell, (1)

Eyes magnetic, pull powerful,
Lips, pinkish petals softly rule,
Earrings, nose pin entangles,
Necklaces, bracelets, bangles, (2)

Waist strings jewelry encircle,
Ringing silver anklet sparkle,
Slim legs, tiny feet, beautify,
Stark beauty, idol girl, signify, (3)

Long nose, penetrating eyes,
Silent idol inviting amplifies,
Look at her singing, dancing,
No love emotions enhancing, (4)

Touched her sense, life tense,
Contemplate, confused, intense,
Mute, deaf, blind in caricature,
Astonish, capable demeanor, (5)

Ringing in mind tells, correct,
Life in a prison chained direct,
Dance baby, ready is dancing,
Playing a part amorous saying, (6)

She dances, sings, laughs a lot,
Idol with hands, lifeless effort,
Amazed got alert, she little cry,
Socked, a whisper, death terrify, (7)

Gleaming bedroom wall paints,
The cushion embroidery scents,
Damsel, fair, hair auburn, curly,
Obeys instantly serves utterly, (viii)

Proposed her ties for a lifetime,
She neither confirms, nods dime,
Clay idol stood motionless rock,
Eyes inert, directly looking, sock, (9)

Go away, sahib, quickly, warning,
A death in front heart churning,
Clay idol turned the day entered,
Human life, years less mustered, (10)

Chain is invisible, death monitor,
Clay idol a life enchants enamor,
Hurt me, love me, play, act idol,
Civilization, mute, ignore symbol, (11)

Civilized decent family men here,
Enjoy, play with an idol, less fear,
Pay money, forget this idol is alive,
Her parents family seldom believe, (12)

Disbelieve his daughter is in danger,
Kidnapped raise hue-n-cries, sheer,
Quit soon, clay idol heart fractured,
No fragrance dream life structured. (13)

Clemency

To err is the human mind trap,
The most powerful one nicely wraps,
Wraps righteous path, a trickster,
Wrong deeds seem right n allure,

Mind spreads a spider net of lust,
The thought gets caught acts most,
From seer to ignorant, all ages,
Females or men fascinate n craze,

Envy, greed, dreams too big soon,
Life adopts the wrong root, a short boon,
Crime does happen by breaking the rules,
Every second it occurs, nor shaken,

The rules followed in time most, get caught,
Art to escape the law, in court well fought,
Clemency to admitting fault in time,
Few reconstruct life discipline fine,

Humanity is awake to a precious life,
Clemency is an award, scope to thrive,
Crime sees anger, greed, jealousy,
Hatred, blind notions, loot property,

Violent minds hurt, kill merciless,
Clemency to culprit heart, crime senseless,
People, in darkness, unaware, do commit,
Crime, once proved clemency permits,

Womanhood is a curse time rewinding,
Child marriage, dowry, bride burning,
Kidnapping, domestic work, slavery,
Illiteracy, in the chain to home treachery,

A crime of civilization for centuries cruel,
Clemency to girl education, skill swells,
The dark age of rule liquidated bride is pride,
Girl grows up as the leader in facets stride,

Social lifts, finance, internet, health,
Clemency has seen social crime to death,
Clemency to cursed life early death,
A modern woman attracts plenty of wealth,

Wealth is not an asset, a means of life most,
Experience, skill, bravery, vision, trust,
Poorest teenager in the dirt, savage, sick,
Centuries back, a cursed life, human tricks,

Deprived of education, health, food, cloth,
The crime of human, slavery, servant,
Runaway, orphan, illicit kid begs pity,
Compassion guides for clemency beauty,

Shelter to the street child, free education,
Health care, nutritious food, the book often,
The child is the future of human life, alert in care,
Clemency to soft rule, caste, poor share,

In ancient myth, the divine ran to golden deer,
His wife got kidnapped, clemency was denied to the seer,
The symbol of truth (Judhistira), the right path, erred once,
Played a dice game blind, bet wife at once,

Denied clemency for an enlightened, banished,
Clemency got opaque, the royal race vanished,
A murdered approached sage to kill, loot,
The sage told his sin, the family refused fruit,

An ignorant realized pleaded for clemency,
Advised to utter Divine name Rama ecstasy,
Years to a decade, killer rant name in reverse,
Continuous "Mara" changed to name endorse,
A sage wrote Ramayana (Valmiki), clemency duly,
Clemency denied kings of two ages discreet,
Turn a murder to sage to cleanse, complete.

CLIFFHANGER

The beginning

The saga of rejection a spirit vows rare,
The realm in the ecstasy of dreams joy share,
The paradise on earth myriads of bondage,
The tears smile fun sweet in pain in phase,
Sorrow worries, fear torture, the mind in silence,
Swap life for pleasure, peace state luminance,
Childhood youth, adult family life in stages,
Thrills temptations in studying career knowledge,
Birds of the same feather fly in the sky in hope, as if to sail,
Bondage new generation, commoner rolls on the rail,

The REDEMPTION in prison

One bird cross, fly over a cliff wall for the realm,
Never returns to greens surrender to the unknown,
The intense urge in my mind, a detached heart,
Love solitude, silence, nature with self-effort,
Rejection of childhood and parental attachment,
School life book friends game n fun lament,
The sweet home pull extreme cut-off, link,

Moves sudden distant destination wink,
The path never traveled, even foot sinks,
Temptations of human life whisper in love,
O' soul human life, the rarest pious involve,
Duty to parents aging community waits,
Human responsibility lies in life procreation,
Family children have new hope for the future,
Wife or husband is the rarest love suture,
Never take steps to cut off the thread of life,
Emancipation treads on a flower, not on the knife,
Every step do listen, feet on thorn a test,
Sorrow, pain, illness, hunger, strike anger, infest,
Peace and calmness vanquish at the conjugal nest,
Return home shed dejection won life n breed,
Freedom lies, in essence, serves people as a seed,
Entices bondage of life stuff human love,
The ascetic acerbic mind turns mute call dissolves,
Fragile limbs move ahead far from humanity,
Climb the stiff curves of a pedestrian path to the cliff,

REDEMPTION enamor free of bondage

Hunger weakness hunted frame severe, in the cold,
The inert body lays still thought with wings of fire,
Hover on the cliff in state cliffhanger sunlight gold,
The heart turns detached, eyes closed, mind in surrender,
Wreck my soul, O Lord, I seek you as a goal, secure,
You can destroy this mortal frame, not me,
Liberate from this dungeon spirit, deathless, I mean,
In footpath days pass in the first test of mind,

Immense energy and freshness in life return rekindles,
Slopes bend hairpins higher to altitude in devotion,
A human spirit uncommon climb, distant commotion,
In quest of an unknown for the mind creator invisible,
Life in silence, lonely nature care permissible,

REDEMPTION on the precipice

Alas, the traveler sleeps in meadows on the green carpet,
Stars in the night turn bed lamp gentle breeze swept,
Moonlight cool caress a divine frame firefly hymn,
Morning rays warm pinch to awaken soul shine,
Cliff fountain cool clearly nourishes a thirsty heart,
Nature lovers and shelter spirits in elements in the dirt,
Know the detached mind of the soul now a fortress,
Brings damsels new infinite beauty to impress,
Captured in temptation spirit slips on a slope,
Back to amorous people trembles sagging hope,
Not those spirits have the destiny to die in ascension,
Continue to rise high on the path of rejection,
The next stage comes fear hunted manifold cruel,
Great O' soul by calm mind prayer luminous swell,
Dispels darkness, fear acts on ignorance well,
Light of the soul, the sole knowledge inner, crumble, quell,

REDEMPTION concludes cliffhanger

The time of final hour trials crumpled by will,
Spirit finds a path and terminates on top of the cliff,
The horizon paradise of the Lord extends infinite,

The soul witnesses impassion standstill,
Down at one side mundane world of joy in pain,
Another side, a gentle slope, flower beds, a fountain,
Almighty shines brighter than Sun yet soothes,
The spirit leaves the limbs like bird moves,
The ultimate state of soul death must die,
The illusion of earth to the seer looks, in owe
The cliffhanger climax to the realization divine saw.

Cocoon

A day heart celebrates an unforgettable one,
Decades back, tiny this heart thirsty did plan,
A teenage life study was a distant dream,
Forest flower fragrance sweet pity ever seen,
Early age, huge funds in need seeking knowledge,
Never remember hours and days counted for a college,
Knew passion in mind beyond reaching a goal,
Once sat at a beach near home, prick for path soul,
Tears of helplessness did sweep churn earning heart,
A gentle breeze from the sea kissed cool whispers an art,
(1)

Never guess one clue reveals adopting a cocoon,
A study by day writes overnight to read a lot soon,
Returned home spun silvery threads of a lesson,
A table, the lantern burned insight nightlong session,
Reminiscence heavy-heart the golden day in a haze,
Never looked back in life, dreams got colors in phases,
School life pre-college over left far off for higher aims,
Penniless, I moved into a venture where it will persist, (2)

There is a way, help I got in time,
Grew as a budding engineer in frontier technology fine,
On a memorable day, I left my Alma Mater degree, I did shine,
Testing year's incredible nights, glue on table n lamp,
Evening faded to midnight, and dawn curious life plan,
Most intricate complex Logic innovate my solutions,
Hour's long effort Perceptive thoughts seek involution,
All sped fast, a day left the hostel efforts endless melt,
Night bus window I sat, alert, warm tears a smile dwelt,
Life trod way to be addressed by my world as an engineer,
Loved the table lamp Or lantern and the wooden chair sheer,
A cocoon of my life Ignorant mind pupa metamorphoses,
Alma Mater loving damsel transforms cocoon transpose,
The technology threads silken woven grew the insight,
Came out an engineer well-spun time of harsh summer,
Passed life hibernated in a cocoon that is institute IIT, (3)

Dreams of life soon at Cocoon graced higher studies,
Bid adieu in a year after life passed as a golden service,
Found room as a cocoon, ever the cell is comfortable in light,
Table n chair in flair service life this mind,
Yarn silken tech-works share day sank in the east,
Too late evening a room works are life so I,
Surprised the day I quit soon, a date for my life passed,
On a cocoon, on a table, the desktop is my window,
To the world keeps me stable, I stay in my Cocoon, (4)

In days of lockdown, the day cocoon ejects me,
Contemplate, look at the veil, and it is felt the last day,
Here leave a cocoon for good love lifelong a tiny wrap,
That protected well my realm wonderful spirit,
A place in the big world I swell the engineers' day,
My love song on Cocoon, a heart today walk,
In memory lane, alone, O' my sweet Cocoon,
A bundle of roses I offer an engineer's gratitude today,
A marvel in my life, you did transform me every day. (5)

Colors

Discovered the root mind colored,
Matches entity lives spring colored,
Colored wings of butterflies or birds,
Colorful sky at dawn and at dusk,

Colorful season blossoms spread happiness,
Looked at my world, colors impressed,
Who sprinkles willfully color dust,
Greeneries, brown hills, blue lakes,

Plants inherit colored leaves stem,
Animal fish living beings pattern,
Color pattern infinite why inked,
The subtle awareness world fascinates me,

The root in mind colored nature,
Varied bright color characters emit,
Humans love, eyes compassionate,
Caring at heart serves people a lot,

Treat sick patients waking in the night,
Sympathetic life prayer, quick recovery,
Lo laborers work hard to build the country,
Pittance they get on return, simple life,

Fewer their grudge anger, frustration,
Seen peace and happiness in their eyes,
Infectious their smiles, innocence lit,
Seen teachers educate children honestly,

Meager income, modest life, truthful,
Imbibe knowledge, skill, talent, humility,
Observed generations, stories emulate
Peasant, his father, child, grand kind,

Follow professions, feed the people,
Extracting privilege not in their heart,
Bargain for modest life amid nature,
Happiest people, hard work helping,

The nurse, postman, watchman, police,
Doctors, artists, painters, writers, actors,
Intricately juxtapose passion supreme,
Alacrity touched my heart no ambition,

Sacrifice personal desires whimsical,
Job is the supreme duty to entertain lives,
Serve the sick and in danger, bring news,
Lack of haughty spirit boast arrogantly,

The silent mass, builders' ingenuity,
Build building road construction a lot,
Takes trouble, fewer questions bluntly,
Shoulder inhuman tasks time bar rings,

Round the day and night, miss family,
Forgot personal life luxury pleasure,
Speechless to notice these colorful lives,
The world today around us is colored brightly,

Safe and happy humans and citizens,
Astonished at their dances festivals,
Spraying colors, painted faces, tainted dresses,
Night for light sparks happiness lost,

The greetings, gifts, and sweet shops open,
Enjoyed smiles of hurt and wounded,
Forget the missing dear ones hunting,
Infects festive occasions rebuild strength,

Look at the future hope, aspiration,
Seen folk weep and beg to Lord a lot of idols,
Ornate these temples with colored lamps lit,
Garland decorates the Lord, soaked prayers,

A profusion of color Lord's abode like a lamp,
Burning bright spectral light refracted,
Below the lamp, darkness stays vivid,
Failed light of the lamp to eliminate,

Evil lives in mind dark and gruesome,
Harbor cruelty, greed, jealousy, anger,
Sad my world dual duality performs,
Chose suitable color warmth storm,
Chose death devil behind the black rose,
Fascinated drunk, and divinity rose.

Compulsion

Thoughts myriad sweep provoke,
Floored an unruly heart, life to revoke,
Witness mind plays naughty link,
Blows the candle lighted rethink, (1)

Ushers darkness imagination lit,
Freedoms follow dreaming delight,
Fascinate object allures intoxicate,
Whispers emotions communicate, (2)

Aspiration endless suffocate wild,
Reminds memory, illusions mild,
Blue planet crimson skies invite,
Asset grab quickly lifelong excite, (3)

Study more burns midnight lamp,
Career prostrates before revamp,
Like doctors, serve people, a surgeon,
Save life runs knife is a profession, (4)

Amused grateful eyes speechless,
Hands folded tears, lives impress,
Revamp the idea, life of an engineer,
T square drawing board act peer, (5)

The pencil-drawn picture of a tower,
Tomorrow to stands sky scrapper,
A million lives work here day-night,
Unknown the engineer drew right, (6)

Stood the towering glory of decades,
He built bridges, dam barricades,
Immortal the pencil paper divider,
Engineer life imaginative provider, (7)

Cancel spirit decide to be a pleader,
Fight in court bend laws bewilder,
Win culprit owes innocent crowd,
Lo black gown devil's wizard loud, (viii)

Scratch everything allures a pilot,
Learn flying planes, the world is pivot,
Watch the ocean and continent below,
Gadgets of colored lights in a hallow,(9)

Guide the plane carry passengers,
Night sky star-studded with dangers,
Safely pilot to a destination in time,
Fulfillment of dream, life is divine, (10)

Students and the teacher interacted,
Passed students the school indicated,
A thousand avenues hope to awaken,
Hugged all tearfully my children, (11)

Not student loved from my heart,
Build spirits burn candle impact,
Face my country, youth depending,
Askance deep hurt chain breaking, (12)

Lead the sacred land in front, hail,
Clean life uncorrupt dare to assail,
There my children bring prosperity,
Usher the golden era skills reality, (13)

Stood silently, students leave school,
Compulsion human heart time fool,
Who struggles, grabs opportunities,
Time acts as luck, fate possibilities, (14)

A mere teacher I looked, my palm,
Compulsion, tendered buds, calm,
Life single, mine no family, chosen,
Lighted candles, many lives frozen. (15)

Camaraderie

Unseen amalgam in the offing,
A capital of billion plus people,
Escaped out of slavery, freedom,
Scintillating democracy stable, (1)

Astonishing fraternity cohesive,
Hundreds of languages, dialects,
The platform of all religions is vibrant,
Dismantled caste creeds sight, (2)

Equal rights constitution fight,
The chasm of gender closed feat,
Emancipated womanhood treats,
Education equal right bestowed, (3)

Strength, feminine, strong roared,
Youth innovative, skilled, literate,
Confidence visible land debate,
Unity solemn promise prospers, (4)

Nation first, nation building vowed,
Fractures animosity, suspicion,
Society, once torn apart, now scorn,
Hate corruption exploitation fight, (5)

Election cleans administration.
The occasion country guides the world,
Pronounced leadership forward,
Global views appreciate the honor, (6)

The capital of the nation is decorated,
Country leaders powerful, converge,
Proclaim peace doubts submerge,
The bond will be streamlined well, (7)

Innumerable glitches to be ironed out,
The summit untying knots express,
Frame clauses acceptable rule press,
Facilitate economy commerce travel, (viii)

Solve critical factor time encounters,
Frame futuristic rules signed news,
Spread like wildfires statements,
Blaze over the globe leaders face, (9)

Acclaimed, applauded, forgotten soon,
Fades the sighed paper time culprit,
Allies inimical suspicious verbatim,
Interpretation will differ extremely, (10)

Still, humanity expects bonhomie,
Earnestly, humanity dreams of fraternity,
Urges the world to build friendship, amity,
Leaders in one city, discussion dinner, (11)

Sideways meets bridge relationship,
Remind the framework for decades,
The moment the world united stay together,
Hope world find peace prosper, (12)

Eliminate war, mend nature, fragile,
Find clues to meet climate, hostile,
They will come with guards, cars,
Book top hotels security in alert, (13)

Closed the capital city lives blocked,
Ordinary life watch telecast awed,
Leaders, they arrive, meet, depart,
Camaraderie visible feeble impact, (14)

Hang me or clap bona fide glamour,
One world, one family, one future...
Camaraderie visible virtual royal,
Smiles, hugging, handshake regal. (15)

Concur

A stubborn heart dictates aroused,
Synchronizes mind all actions,
Doubt, if, but all creep, sabotage,
An enemy from birth soul cries,

Suspect strange world unknown,
Faces looking amused, surprised,
From perennial darkness to light,
A child is born light captives instantly,

Human belief, the radiance divine,
Encounter that instant vanishes,
Noises, touch, food mold slowly,
The blaze is forgotten, trivialized,

This light exists within perfectly,
Experienced in life from children,
Shining their eyes gleaming face,
Sparkling teeth amid dark hair,

Often witness tears reflect light,
Radiates emotion thought silently,
Light provides warmth, hugs kids,
Warmth shared my heart probing,

How come life radiates warmth,
A light that divine existence stays,
Watched rivers brimming full,
Spate flooding waters breached,

Breached the embankment, strong,
Changes rive in the season to sand bed,
The arrogance, pride, mindless no more,
Quiet, serene blue waters project,

Muddy waters whirlpool swirling,
Astonished mind exhibits doubtful,
Overwhelm heart trusting light,
Shows condense to gathering cloud,

Reject creation, control of the master,
Wishes actuate, automatic, negated,
Not at all substantive to surrender,
A human mind can fight to withstand,

Control elements as the desired mend,
To productive resources and output,
Defy the invisible power goad element,
Ingenuity intelligence thinking unites,

Recreate, hypothetically, hypocrisy,
Artificial intelligence, devised by humans,
Perform like a human or excel further,
Where is this light and warmth within?

Stops their philosophy completely,
The periphery of matter science light exists,
Light exists in Sun, moon, or Earth,
Lighted universe galaxies, stars,

The cumulative light is candlelight,
Lighted by myself, oil lamp burning,
Same is this phenomenon feature,
Close my eyes image duly glimmers,

Mind is a mirror, reflects perfectly,
Accurate if is an image opposite,
Strike thoughts into mind mysterious,
The soul within is a reflection of light,
This light is from an oil lamp lit brightly,
Crumbling disbelief fades doubt soon,
Concur life is a burning candle or boon.

Confess A Canvasser

Election rural opportunity

Life never means leisure idle,
Work uplifts life inertia riddle,
School, college studies needle,
Examination results in the middle,
Food shelter needs job bridle,
Luxuries comfort needs fiddle,
Award rewards in knowledge,
At least life opts to seek privilege,
College degree, the title of bachelor,
Claim proudly passes n smile,
Apply n apply no reply, a job,
Fruitless to plead one in sobs,
Harsh a life family hurt many,
Money is sweeter than honey,
Discover a life of vendor sweet,
Carry goods to villages, meet,
Meet people who bargain cheaply,
Simple folk buy benefits to reap,
The life of the vendor is a meager income,
Confess canvasser works won,
Election time candidate offers,

Distribute voter list vouchers,
The voucher lists the candidate party,
Canvassing vending is beauty,
Life acquired villager address,
Name age family member yes,
Welcome election good income,
Confess a canvasser handsome, (1)

From grass root to leadership

The story does not end short here,
Rose from grassroots in a year,
A familiar face in a rural region,
People trust mix in years own,
Political life influential benefit,
Convey people information with,
Bring rural people information,
Life of canvasser bridle wisdom,
Electoral success or defeat lace,
Confess a canvasser wins a race,
Victory brings power to a leader,
Life of a canvasser meant a lot secure,
Political ladder step luck n fate,
Destiny, work, friendly help vet,
Gossip-rumor create-negate mix,
Local leadership mass base fix,
Less education career, a life open,
Grow canvasser leader newborn,
Love of people, faith, life turns pink,
Confess canvasser, betrayal sink. (2)

Confiscate Agonies

Night entangles me, dreams me enchant,
Remember the youth and dream merchant,
Rebellious heart, wild mind suffocate,
Desires spread wings thrill intoxicate, (1)

Passion fuels young limbs to seek season,
An Earth in bridal dress enamor vision,
Crimson rays at dawn, warm thought,
Sterile mind invigorate realm wrought, (2)

Nostalgic a time hunts me in verdure,
Foliage curious mind forest, hill, river,
Wild mind imagine beautiful brook nit,
Mimic flowing hairs of a female if greet, (3)

Gentle wind replicates soft caress love,
Wild creeper flowers blossom flies dove,
Dove, my soul mesmerized youth tease,
Imaginary love stalks bridal dress guise, (4)

Assumes her fragrance jasmine feels shy,
Dews laden lily smiles, drink lips bit try,
Try n succeed convinces if tears of love,
Deem night in etching encounter her to solve, (5)

Enchanting beauty descends, company,
Never forget these night swell encounters,
Romance flood feeling in mist disappear,
Dawn breaks swell emotion self laments,
Agonies sweep my mind, her charms current, (6)

Queen of heart from an unknown land visit,
Pain, misery, a wound of life erases, discreet,
Heals her potion of love nectar n elegant,
Decade water flew under the bridge rant, (7)

Immaculate her dress, infectious, smile lip,
Rejuvenate sterile heart memories creep,
Numerous queries arise where love exists,
Must be her land a paradise enwrap mist, (viii)

I believe a land sans illness, agony, pain,
Little war, hatred, cruelty, anger, yet rain,
Peaceful landscape of her heavenly abode,
Mysteries shroud profound hopes erode, (9)

Land of kind heart, merciful, care n serve,
In dreams confiscate agonies, all dissolve,
Tearful melancholic song of romance test,
Ripe age a time Corona spread n bitterest, (10)

My land cries owe none to listen to crumble,
A million souls gasp for a breath never be simple,
Death roams like a predator day and night equal,
Happiness peace forgot safe vaccine wall, (11)

Jovial children never giggle, fear, tension hit,
Ends my song tragic aspires my love if, meet,
Feel to greet her profusely weave intarsia nit,
Weave in sweet dreams again n doubt invite,
I would welcome her confiscate agonies here,
If taken me to her abode, heal my land secure. (12)

Confluence Of Couture

Incredible beauty nature invites,
River, mountain, and forest excite,
Immobilize serenity often charms,
A people simple and mingles warms, (1)

Tribal young females, their smiles,
Costume, ornaments, attire style,
Youth reflects rapids swell move,
A joyous time love intimacy wove, (2)

Youths, male and female dancers, ecstatic,
Amazingly a visit imprints romantic,
Dark hair on young women's curve,
Curves of the ravine attract serve, (3)

Exotic female voices saturate the song,
Green forest fragrant flowers long,
Mesmerizes my heart mingle sure,
Pulsating dances of youth enamor, (4)

A rhythm confluence with the step,
Beatings of the drum love life help,
Remember my dances, drink thrill,
Reverberates forest n vibrates hill, (5)

Waves surge in young hearts like,
Waves of swollen river flow alike,
Scents of wildflowers worn by girls,
Magnetic their pull if a lust snarls, (6)

Silence of night dark forest recall,
Nostalgic lusty heart, discover all,
Rain-soaked greens attract again,
Mingle with tribal people, remain, (7)

Wet earth aroma smells infectious,
Infectious boundless joy onerous,
Purity of nature fresh, wind, water,
Simple people, unforgettable jeer, (viii)

Hunt forest animal fruit, root all,
Lunch, dinner, morning, dusk call
Obscure a village of mud cottages,
Weaver of cloth pattern,n envisages, (9)

Colorful natural ingredients rich,
Tribal design art mimics lives, each,
Lives in pen, unique n wonderful,
Saree for women weave incredible, (10)

Simple cotton yarns, natural color,
A confluence of couture, exotic culture,
Nine yards of cotton hand-printed,
Appreciate world women n excited, (11)

Real feelings compared with textiles,
Technology urban couture in exiles,
Realized cottage products are priceless,
Tribal design pattern arts impress, (12)

Festival nearer, I bought beautiful prints,
Offers to my family present mints,
Dresses elegant festive atmosphere,
Confluence couture n tribal culture, (13)

Conjure Up Sonnet

Precious life fades premature,
Knowledge skill age recapture,
Recapture past troubles tame,
Recapture life takes root in fame,
Recounts endless agonies end,
Remember courage, belief lend,
Reconstruct life in ruins treat,
Resolve discipline hopes greet,
Reconnect past valor fight tuff,
Revive glorious present in a huff,
Rotate cycles of sorrow, peace,
Reunite spirits, supreme bliss,
Revise evil nature, anger, greed,
Retains love, compassion to heed, (1)

Relents humiliation, heart hurt,
Relentless to forgive, forget lust,
Recover crumpled ego humble,
Resound victory of life trample,
Repeat ruthless, cruel crumble,
Redress prides desires rumble,
Restart, sprinkle calmness swell,

Redraw tranquil mind cares a nail,
Remit past sin suffer n awaken,
Revisit paradise on earth detain,
Return to abode conquer hornet,
Rewrite life conjure up a sonnet,
Reinstate indomitable spirit call,
Rejoice in secure life, inspires soul, (2)

Replay sonata of progress power,
Replicate divine grace trust pure,
Readmit hidden treasure within,
Recollect conscience intellect win,
Research realm of illusion remold,
Rediscover truth eternally, and behold,
Realign orderly life truth to pervade,
Resurrect soul realizes light invades,
Recoils deeds store in memory all,
Rekindle light within memory roll,
Remind a sojourn birth-death toll,
Revisit world satiate hunger recall,
Realize hunger fire desire fuel mix,
Retreat from evil nature wisdom fix, (3)

Ravages my life, savage instinct,
Rotates bitter battle win distinct,
Revert moral character succeeds,
Reassess ignorance slowly recedes,
Reenter opulence of virtue strong,
Rebound detach prejudice wrong,
Redirect messages sufferers heal,

Rejuvenate human believers kneel,
Remorse pain illness scares amiss,
Reveal new period my dream wish,
Recalibrate student studies are different,
Resurrect 21st-century man to invent,
Retains friendship amity rise unity,
Delink death destruction war does exist, (4)

Remarket destiny, fate, fortune, luck,
Next century humans find saga sock,
New dawn after century promulgate,
Conjure up sonnet life in tears melt (5)

Connect

Once upon a time, happens to be a chick,
Cries of this baby reverberated alarmed,
The entire family knew the baby, hungry,
Soiled the cloth limbs smeared less angry,

There was the mother cleaned you well,
Feed from her breasts smiles quell,
The giggling playful arms and legs, a sight,
The tiny one once started crawling was news,

The day child walks celebration at home,
Calling papa Mama the musical rare to find,
It was this youth, Big Bird, that fled,
Wings wide, he spread happily left a shore,

The shore of the home grew up, studied,
Earned awards after awards certificates,
The civilized world embraced this soul,
Do earn, do learn, be born as a citizen,

The soil, today missing dearly wind and water,
The grain field golden shed waving sad,
The greeneries hill mountain cast sorrows,
Left children her soil flight above oceans,

Nested in far-off countries, prospered well,
The people noticed migrants wise dwell,
Time watched everything, silent witness,
Eternal music is time, story hundreds,

Back at home, the woman's hair is graying,
Whitish patches increasing life depict,
Wrinkles now visible, limbs tired but quiet,
Deep within her heart, still burning love,

My child, my child, his name exceeds,
What exceed dear human than Allah,
More than Jesus, Lord, Krishna but dear,
Exists in this life to pray for safety, security,

Worship sharp on the birthday of her child,
Prays now to the unseen Lord for his long life,
Never demanding, less tell her service,
Love, only glowing love alive subtly touch,

Come on baby, an adult now feel strong,
An established man confident so wrong,
The blood flowing in your vein her gift,
Forgot the umbilical cord connects the navel,

The womb, once sheltered for nine months,
Allowed the baby to travel the globe,
Urban modern life O' busy, extremely busy,
Works day and night to fight for the future,

Promotion, bright career, money, golden,
What not I achieved in life ego boasting,
Applaud children and sweet darling,
Gifts plenty showered hugged family,

Today this man fell sick, fevers rising,
The disease is less severe bedridden for a week,
Dead of the night, wake up suddenly,
Surprised, silent night, home is in darkness,

All switches switched off his wife sleeping,
Who made him get up surreal,
Next dawn, his wife answered him,
You were shouting Ma, Ma, Ma, continuous,

Thought you were dreaming she slept,
Not slept in another part of the globe,
Someone profusely sweating got up,
Her worried face trembling every fiber,
Connect with the cord, dear human,
From the navel to early home, the womb!

Continental Bird

Introspect once the nesting ground is far off a place,
Stood still hours on the roof, a single streak in grace,
Sailing as a gentle cloud of white glistens under the Sun,
The beak, tail, wings wide, transfix cover light,

Sun percolate bypassing white feathers, a song,
Misses among clouds move fast from the haze,
Immersed in emotions, in heart, what spirit flies,
Far below a mundane world corona eclipse fry,

Death threat the human spirited across the continent,
The incredible sight stole my heart, replicates divine,
Horizons shy the being traces earth a borderline,
High altitude soars forward passage of time define,

Unaware of agonies, fear, tensions tear far below,
Lush green forest, sky, kissing hills, rivers serpentine,
All must be visible, but little humans soar,
Lost in thought if the mighty bird happier than me,

Surely it knows the essence of freedom pass on borders,
No missile fighter planes target the gait tears,
Wishes to descend anywhere in the globe fetches goodwill,
A cliff of marshy water bodies in mid-forest rest at will,

Looked up the white being crossing the ocean smoothly
Alone flies high above giant waves fill amazed dizzy,
The migration ends alien a place unknown birds feed,
Few in flock few en-mass rest solitary stranger,

Returns after months of journey family flew away,
A colony it knows shifts as clouds in seasons,
Wander struck, and now I sat introspect all within,
How similar my soul with this mighty bird shines,

Never aware life is gone, stay only accompany me,
Passage of time does happen the silvery spirit soars,
Alone a journey as an arrow high up in the sky,
The earth underneath forgets the travel oceans will be shy,

Freedom my soul acquire as the mighty wings,
Cross mountains, clouds, forest deserts all the same,
No barrier, no hatred, fights, or love in the trace,
Impassion a state like this being quit identity time,

Felt cool and calm in bliss shivering cold breeze,
Someone whispers deep in me, deathless in the biz,
Far subtle the being my soul soar to void,
Timeless afloat, no attributes state of mind motionless,

Alone who knows it may exist in a home voiceless,
Instinctive divine wish the mighty bird will descend,
New life world differ name known faces a home,
The feeding ground of migratory birds on wisdom,
Left my roof thinking the scene of the flying spirit sublime,
Migrate the continental bird in time.

COWERED

Fascinating a life takes pride most,
Translates life hard-work unfailingly,
Saw childhood modest home parents,
Happy, their dreams, son excelled in studies,
With minor education, my mother watched,
Time established, talents of her son, happy,
Tears offered to Lord had been listening,
Prayers of a passionate mother fulfilled,
Her child, established and famous, rich in life, (1)

Her nine-yard cloth hand-woven, bangles,
Vermilion dot on her forehead, covered,
Happiness knew no boundary to get a letter,
Reverberates sound ma non-existent, feeling,
Read through letter after letter of a dear child,
His meteoritic rise in life, if unbelievable,
Her gratitude for a picture of the Lord bowed,
Begging mercy, a long life, safety, and happiness,
Wife, children of her son, grow, by grace,
Her world, she knows by heart, her son,
Son's family visited his parent's home years later, (2)

Mother's homemade cakes, food, delicious,
Tired her each limb, she did not care,
Fed her child, grandkids, daughter-in-law,
Dirty floor, broken windows, spider nets,
Turn bed sheet, old wooden bed cracking,
Toilet in the backyard with a brick wall,
The jackfruit tree is laden with a hundred,
Grassy courtyard, moss everywhere,
Wooden hearth, smoky, carbon-coated wall,
Cement floor, the son was relishing dishes,
Granddaughter cried, sighting cockroach,
A cat jumped playful, mewing,
Children demanded to return, the family left, (3)

Mother was looking through the door,
The car went out of sight, and she was standing,
Her husband, now old enough, was coughing,
Bedridden, it was medicine time,
Her husband inquired about the visit to her son,
About their request for treating his father,
She was caressing his bony legs, crying,
Silent, hidden under the veil of cloth,
She left soon after the bed,
And heard her husband calling, (4)

Querying, has my son invited us?
Has he assured me of my treatment?
I don't want to die here, feverish in pain,
Mother was thinking, she told her son,
To take his father to medical for treatment,

Yet her child was pretending never heard,
She knew the rejection, deathly silence,
Her child never looked at his father, gone!
She was feeding her husband, heard,
What son was telling, in my case?
She only cowered and prayed to the Lord,
This time praying for her husband,
At the feet of the wooden idol, she was crying,
Maybe Lord himself felt cowered… (5)

CREATION.

The mind is the world itself,
The question comes but known,
From teenage to ripe ages,
Trillions such have come n gone,

Self-solved by mind and inquisitive,
The same is mind probed n found the most,
Life gave challenges, mind took all,
Solved as it could but failed to,

Birth to death is knowledge,
Souls even carry forward,
Next life, intuition leads to darkness,
Of consciousness, it is my thought,

It goes on n on for the mortal world,
And beyond, but even I couldn't find, who am I?
From where I came n shall return,
Remain unanswered lifelong,

when I see this picture n questions,
Hello world, please say to me the answer,
Looked a second, and it came to me,
A whisper in utter silence,

I heard as if the mind tells,
The eternal truth,
Neither has a beginning nor an end,
CREATION.

Credence

The truth of universal motherhood is explicit,
Ocean, skies, and earth reflects her discreet,
Her womb is ocean life began its journey,
Her creation is creatures, animals many,

Bird, aquatic life sings her glories are free,
Lush green forest, waterfalls, ravines n trees,
All whisper credence to her creation magic,
Mother erases in times credence to tragic,

Her heart is divine love creation grows new,
Death is a cleansing process when birth renews,
Eon saw species grow on earth, joy grew,
Mother changes all, new lives roam and earth,

Evolution gives credence to a better life, worth,
Her dedication, intricate is a human being,
An intelligent mind understands everything,
Mother empowers the human mind with both,

One is delusion in dark attitude relish,
Entraps soul to a prison of the earth in blemish,
Torture and hurdles in life awaken mortal,
Escapes beguiling mind detaches total,

Mother smiles, her play a child wins,
Her blessings gods aspire, a child shines,
Credence of Mothers act to the net as fish,
A child hides under feet, net ever miss,

Enlighten one knows surrender saves,
Elusive realm, others are swept in waves,
Credence confuses mind, life is naïve,
Greed, lust, temptation, and anger are her bait,

Swarming children in hook, till exit wait,
Dark mind is opaque, Mother plays fine,
Invisible and silent, Her creation refines,
Resurrections of Her presence clean,

Dark minds perish, humanity celebrates,
Lights in lamps and hymns in prayer indicate,
Credence to her arrival removes ignorance,
In suffering, fear empowers endurance,

Prays for a tortured soul, and may Mother lead right,
Credence turns to creed, and inner desires fight.
Credence puzzled mind, the mother is left alone,
Lifelong, a soul grows in her sweet home,

Mother languishes in a shelter, sick n sorrow,
Fear, the human mind learns mother tomorrow,
Credence to celebrate prayer to Mother to refine,
Animals love, mothers vegetarian or canine,
Divine Mother to mother's spirit bless same,
A dark mind pretends love credence a name.

CRESTFALLEN CRETIN

Confess life in shatter result,
Pretense adopts faces tumult,
Peril invites attempt, enamor,
Erroneous mind trap secure, (1)

Misguides spirit gold inflame,
Bitter fight grab-wealth tame,
Hook-by-crook accrues assets,
Addict adventure fuel pretext, (2)

Portray to the world innocent,
A benevolent heart helps decent,
Squander plenty, build image,
Reputation design craft craze, (3)

Laugh heartily worlds believe,
Guise intension claim receive,
Amazes lies, people trust total,
Exploit, suffer, console mortal, (4)

Help sufferer peanut proclaim,
Serve humanity, dedicate aim,
Elaborate clear, rise spiral, wit,
Pretend gentle soul ethics writ, (5)

Hit zenith a famous, poor root,
Manipulates a world under boot,
Admire, applaud, feel sympathy,
Deceive wiser, drama empathy, (6)

Award reward accolade amuse,
Sultan of a dark kingdom ruse,
Listens to life builds an empire,
Greed rage least hesitates, dare, (7)

Seen enough, cruel rule spirit,
Mask-faces smiles, yet in discreet,
Luxury comfort opulence craze,
Year's smooth maneuvers haze, (viii)

Bedroom glass wall fearful, lot,
Ugly ghosts reside behind n hurt,
Crude smile, mischievous threat,
Arouses sight of a grave, create, (9)

Look, maleficent predates in sleep,
Wake, cry-loud lone hunts deep,
Fear own face-masks n terrorize,
Adulthood creeps, an age precise, (10)

Paranoia pervades blood cell sink,
Reminiscence reminds deeds link,
See victim disbelief, plead mercy,
The mirror shows eyes, little courtesy, (11)

Sock to watch lifeless eyes burn,
Earn money, earn power, lovelorn,
Boast mighty deceive, credit win,
Crestfallen cretin, guilt tear twin, (12)

Imprisons dungeon build indeed,
Crumple, aspire, ego, hate, deed,
Futile repentance, fail path clear,
In vain, try, pray Lord, disappear, (13)

Sweet home n citadel of evil is a wish,
Serpent of own deeds, amok hiss,
Death, knock loud fear, disappear,
Fail; see the image of a heart somber, (14)

Snakes within reptiles hiss, silent,
Tear dries up sock fizzle, resilient,
Commit a crime, robbery, cheat, fail,
Precious life never return, wit nail, (15)

The mortal frame goes inert, loses total,
Carries sin result wait to repent royal,
Admit open to people beg to forgive,
Crestfallen cretin naïve, pens leave. (16)

CREVASSE

Hostile earth in the coldness of death,
Cracks, limitless length, no breadth,
The depth is unknown n the dark bottom,
Life fell, never escapes, death if, welcomes,

A crater of horror, time seems still,
Eon, time fell in a crevasse, recover uphill,
Pushed to the brink of oblivion, a human deed,
Civilization at zenith collapses quickly indeed,

Nature restarts time in a crevasse n a design,
Erased entire living forms, never life resign,
Time is deathless, sees drifting, crater wide,
Ages pass in turbulence, but again a life ignites,

Million years roll human breaths first,
Evolutes in phases, civilization to last,
Human most intricate creation, the best,
Evil entraps wisdom, crumples till infest,

Time imprisoned in a crevasse, nature rules,
Humans turn into an animal simple, life cool,
The ingenuity of the mind saves time with progress,
Repeated instances etched distress,

Current time humans soar at the peak of power,
History waits for an impatient repeat in an hour,
In sixty minutes, a species obliterate the globe,
Time will find in crevasse, no one to sob,

The human mind is a darkness n intelligence tool,
Capable can vaporize and architect marvels cool,
Million will perish in minutes, no offense,
Time will move swiftly to neutralize defense,

Crevasse waits human conscience entrap,
The powerful n advanced people enwrap,
Evil acts of disease, fever spreads poor,
Enact ethnic cleansing, a conscience to the crater,

A nation with a billion poor in morals,
The spread of the virus, sick people, harassment,
A people with blind hatred for humanity,
Witness dance of death daily insanity,

Conscience in crevasse raises conflict,
The threat of war, pushing pandemic dare,
Invasion, holocaust peace in a nightmare,
Crevasse drifts continent wide in time,

Evil prowls in crevasse life seldom are fine,
Soil, salt, shelter, food, root calls clear,
Hatred pushes to crevasse treason leer,
Festive season cries to lonely sights,

Temples are in lock crevasses delight,
The happiness of the journey to life rues lock,
A caring heart in ruins, selfish shocks,
Time humanity befriended nature,

Simple life, reason alive, love the nurture,
Caring for humanity, sharing others' pain,
Surrendering to almighty wisdom regain,
Realizes the objective of human life is rare,

Unique creation than an animal in bare,
Focus on civilization's pristine glory,
Essence threw to crevasse creator worry,
Time watches quietly, last-minute human,
Globe in crevasse unknown depth began.

Crippiling Exodus

Fortunate soil fosters freedom rare,
Priceless voice less inhibition care,
Chose career to settle, select passion,
Equality golden gift of land motion, (1)

Despite class, creed, religion, best,
Disbelief, the constitution offers perfect,
Ignores speech, color, ethnic races,
Discrimination crime law punishes, (2)

Gender equality, the motto establishes,
Girl education free n distinguishes,
Protect old citizens and the infirm, help the sick,
Moderate finances facility intrinsic, (3)

Sacred land author basic right-best,
Franchises enable voters rightly invest,
Across sections, ban sectarian color,
Ordinary persons choose the leader, (4)

Democratic right, birth, privilege get,
Chose or reject self option intimate,
Right, to earn, study, food n shelter,
None can deny a person live securely, (5)

Peace security, minimum necessity,
Peasants, workers, destitute benefit,
Land provides electricity, school treat,
Health clinics, drinking water meet, (7)

Communication nation provides all,
Air, water, road, travel facility troll,
Born on soil, mingled inhales air, free,
Visit forest, mountain, river, decree, (viii)

Surprises few find the nation intolerant,
Create violence wall hell discordant,
Dismantle willfully, fraternity amity,
People losing self-identity, amity, (9)

Democracy crumbles anarchy exists
Dictators predominate control exhibits,
Mass migration starts sufferers cry,
No future ethnic cleansing new fry, (10)

Peace, asset, home, plunders cruel,
Fragile life crumpled escapes fuel,
Crippling exodus begins world looks,
Glorify incidents help little spooked, (11)

Mass exodus refugee faceless prays,
Rot under open sky life nit dismays,
Lost nationhood without crime run,
Fates, caste, color, faith distinction, (12)

Iron cage encircles discriminate nit,
Extreme views never alone all greet,
Encompass ancient stringent codes,
An open mind, free society, eroding, (13)

Heart-rending appeal pleads mercy,
World-community feels discourtesy,
Revolution to some rebellion victor,
Name of God bloodshed benefactor, (14)

Open sky, foreign soil, wait for a stranger,
Crippling exodus trickle, harbinger,
An era of soil foster, ruthless warning,
Accept subjugation lives rewarding, (15)

Sealed borders n escape impossible,
Listens to sacred hymns; ensemble.
Humanity ponders witness ruckus,
Embrace, assuage, crippling exodus. (16)

Crippled

Exuberance once inflamed the mind,
Devout heart faithful to effort instill,
Born with nothing to boast, proclaim,
Deprivation is invisible, chained tightly,

Hunger, the pang of indescribable hurt,
Roamed through streets with alacrity,
Help O neighborhood help to survive,
Get a morsel of food, can take a breath,

Help me to study at a university, established,
Forget an anonymous birth, sad teenage,
Look, O human, the seed grows a growth,
Few years after hundred feet high luxuriant,

Pregnant with such dreams expectant,
To toil hard on rocky and barren land,
Convinced to harvest and cultivate struggle,
Reject impossibility devoted, really,

A miraculous story of a life through help,
Achieved success, name, and fame,
Rewarded people funded benevolently,
Cured devastated heart to stability,

Stood firmly with men and women in life,
Provided me, a shelter, food, cloth, money,
Selfless their assistance remembered,
At odd hours provided a helping hand,

Saw their children get married and settled,
Used my power position in return,
Felt capable able to pay back,
Debts of their sacrifice for me indebted,

Tearfully provided assets, goods, gadgets,
Savor their grateful eyes happily,
Story not here ended life changed,
Irk of fate turned luck and success,

Left my better half suddenly with kids,
She provided no reason out of the blue,
Missed my home and found a ghost house,
Hunted countless luxuries asset,

What for, for whom, inkling heart,
Not able to weep tears failed miserably,
Silence gripped long lonely hours,
Fear outside world, noise, busiest,

Preferred loneliness dark chamber,
Fail to analyze past, present, and future,
Why did it happen she blocked me,
Thousand earnest pleadings fell flat,

Children choose mother separated,
Angry to think of a past downtrodden,
An illegitimate child orphan once confided,
A Boomerang strike hit me grounded,

She accused me of hiding facts cheating,
Ask my conscience the womb invited,
Never knew a mother would reject a newborn,
Someone kind-hearted took to lap,

Grew up in a poor cottage, but divine heart,
Accepted as my parents, adorned, worshiped,
My family rejected my parents as outsiders,
Decided never to squander my property,

To live to find reclusion and accept lonely life,
A birth not cursed life was precious,
So many people showed kindness,
Never to defeat my fate that posed,

Twilight years longing for happiness, peace,
The setting sun sinking beyond,
Spreading long shadows loves twinkle,
Loved adopted parents loved hearts,

Funded me wholeheartedly, I studied well,
Thanked Lord, successful, rich, and famous,
Touched my skin, on scrutiny, wrinkled,
Rejected an orphan illegitimate crippled!

Crisp Concierge

An enchanting encounter etch,
Life passes gently, a picture fetch,
Search in memory lonely times,
A smiling young girl spread lines,
Her inquiries crisp n modulate,
A guest, young heart confiscate, (1)

She writes swift my replies note,
Her beautiful finger, like a quote,
Golden hair, crisp suit, and polish,
Demeanor her figure waits for relish,
Short time, sweet answer polite,
Fail to guess why lost in delight, (2)

Reluctant, left to my hotel room,
Young heart, but mine amaze soon,
Unknown female myself tourist,
Never got acquainted find tryst,
Her sight beautiful face attracts,
Serene green hills mist distracts, (3)

Life business executive holiday,
Recluse from monotony dismay,
Single in life neatly female friend,
Endless sessions of talk in the end,
Discussions chat outlook forget,
Fail to tantalize, my heart, rivet,(4)

Magnificent city life often travels,
Encounter fair ladies little dwell,
Empty page my life write job well,
Promotion career travel meet nail,
Heart ever seek pick post position,
Never any girl tame heart motion, (5)

The whole night got awake thinking,
New sensations bring the image pink,
Her sweet voice looks seduced state,
Inner equilibrium peace devastates,
The next day found her in talk, in ruin,
She interacts n few n far between, (6)

A group of tourists visits scenic fall,
An opportunity, her company call,
Travels long in forest gossip most,
Mutually got acquainted with my effort,
Last day of the tour concierge greeted me,
Invited her to my office to request it, (7)

An offshore tour challenge project,
Business life hardly could reject,
After a couple of years of hard work and toil,
Promotions package applause swell,
Thought that night her charm float,
Nightlong dream her near almost,(8)

Plan again to visit her place n meet,
Fear yet firm to propose to her n greet,
A conference suddenly blocked travel,
Miseries, endless eager wait unravels,
Just quit the office to take a flight move,
Find crisp concierge newly married,
Her husband greets all plans misfired,
I offered both a hearty dinner night,
Rest of life, a memory sinks delight (9)

Cursed Teenage

O' human, the new age one, ever you saw God,
Reject it, quit these pictures, merciless to bud,
Ever O' soul, divine grace deprived poor kid,
Amazed, Mother Teresa served in love, feeding,

Street children, orphans, poorest ones need,
Great society, forced to beg labor teen, greed,
Heartless ones take their own school, a good dress,
Near home, in shanties the life of a teen, mess,

None cry, heart ever melts, boys toil hard on Sun,
Mother Teresa fed dress, great a shelter home,
A time came to Mother passed out, Jesus welcomed her,
In heaven received her, as Saint Teresa knew,

On this day Anti Child Labor, the world do celebrate,
Street children are bare, hungry, work for cruel fate,
The nation looks away in hate time and asks why fun,
No school life, parentage home nation melts none,

Streets and slum dogs are known! sick, to shiver, lost-n-gone,
East and west, south o north, million labor kids own,

The world asks why O' nations only promise them,
Ever they ask, see the smile, dire in poverty, blame,

God is cruel, born, never they choose, pitted in hell,
Million homes, metropolis, towers, as servant swell,
Humans cruelly and mercilessly treat most in-home as hell,
Ever O' soul saw or keep a servant girl or boy,

Plead today, be graceful, lighten a life n enjoy,
Pledge donations, foundations, growing kids million,
Well food, dress, school life free, serve in love all,
Great, these hearts treat serving poor serving God,

Evils den, divine shine, these spirits are only Lord,
The heart is a swollen river of tears, prays to the Divine,
Only for the sweetest teens, their smiles fun shine,
So innocent, translucent, lives are the same fine,

Lead kingly light to the hearts of people might,
Let these poor children a laborer from plight,
Pray for them, may all as school dress, a sight,
School ground, all teens, playful, laugh n fight,

Well, dressed, nicely fed, storybooks in bed at night,
O God mercifully, no angrier, warm tears bright,
Pray for all these souls, who never can see as light,
Wish my nation to abolish child labor, go height,
Stop misery, death, life rotten, an adult blight,
Today's teen, tomorrow's youth nation proud shake,
Cursed teenage, a life's mirage, nation awake.

Dance Of Deathless

Ageless the civilization of humans,
Invaders through the ages just left no one,
Who stayed ruined culture, faith, traditions,
Raised to dust a large population,

Centuries in a land turned millennium,
Still, a people survive culture as premium,
Rebuilt own citadels of own legacy,
Time has passed, memories were missed,

Spread far n wide, got happy as a nation,
Poverty, disease, hatred cruelty did burn,
The inferno among own shattered peace,
Gone are these golden days smiles they miss,

Hunger, death, suffering, poverty, tears,
Greedy, cruel, sinful beasts among own they fear,
Cataclysmic metamorphosis did happen to tear,
Societies disintegrated into millions of fragments,

Rock-solid walls crept within segments,
Just at this time, humanity got amazed,
A tribe remains untouched and never gets damaged,
The bondage of family, society, community,

Unshackled by resolve, they are beautiful,
What humans understand is family, wealth, and life,
Abolish all from life from teenage yet survive,
Live in a deep forest in solitude or group,

Reject education, modern human outlook,
Love nature, pass life there only,
Learn to survive the search for years solely,
All lust attractions of sensation men only run,

Perish these instincts in detachment n dispassion,
Incredible, they fight this most elusive world,
Imitate the lives of most ancient natives in bold,
Wondering about places in the forest, deep ravines,

Sing alone always the glory of the divine,
They mean to defeat God's house of the mirror,
Reflections of allure pleasure are transient n sure,
Like a dream, it captures, captivates the mind,

A mirror is a mirror act elusive human unkind,
Far from it, trees, rivers, and creatures,
Pass entire life lonely as a creation except for allure,
As the pandemic appeared to spread around the globe,

Death, fear, and busy life stood, Humans but lifeless,
Fail to trust Post Catastrophe, Dance of Deathless !!!!
Never confined, dreaded to unseen the predator,
Unfazed, they roam in the forest loving The Creator.

Dating Moon

Eons human heart found love,
Miseries, pain, sadness absolve,
The depth, bottomless, magical,
Tearful eyes infected, enthrall, (1)

Infectious not disease but love,
Fixed eyes, ears, solitudes solve,
Occupied mind no more lonely,
Intoxicated joyous handsomely, (2)

Dance madly on the road, sing,
Looked at nowhere a wild king,
Plays instruments, lovelorn lit,
In Bus train flight forget greet, (3)

Plays, overwhelms, music mild,
Now tearful, next laughs child,
Auburn hair, curly, torn clothes,
Playing in dusk in park moths, (4)

Fireflies lighting, a hundred stars,
Fullmoon night, single-life scars,
No one in front, behind, tragic,
Milling crowds city lives magic, (5)

Lonely spirit survives eloquent,
Orphan, lost parent, consequent,
Loves strangers, the city people,
Compassionate lives gift simple, (6)

Love children listen to him play,
Laugh at him, cheer steps sway,
Poor, destitute, homeless spirit,
Wait till a full moon, date bright, (7)

Watch the moon silvery, enjoys,
Automatic his songs, playboys,
His dating with the moon is romantic,
Circulates poems song ecstatic, (viii)

His relationship, the moon link,
People record his song yet blink,
Illiterate youth song meaningful,
Thousand poems town watchful, (9)

Quickly published his songs well,
Recordings of his music life hail,
Relate to the moon, lovelorn discreet,
His songs address the moon, hit, (10)

Epitomized as a fairy angelic lit,
Enamored with a single life, explicit,
Washed moonbeams, if abashed,
Love stories moon encompassed, (11)

Inspired people flames spread,
Flame of love moon living read,
Imaginary concept people hate,
Believe his songs, musical date, (12)

Dating moon full moon nights,
Cities broadcast song delights,
News spread Moon Lander irked,
Wild youth crying news pricked, (13)

Shouting plead don't touch my love,
Orbiter on the moon hopes to dissolve,
Existing today the moon source,
Dating moon lovelorn, of course, (14)

Horrified at the scarred surface,
Rock-strewn lifeless to disgrace,
Craters, a dark lunar landscape,
Silent mute his life and sadly escape. (15)

Daughters

Etched in the heart a moment,
Distinct that lasted a lifetime, vivid,
The birth of a daughter fulfilled a dream,
Wordless to coin a word, emotions,

Father's heart, those seconds unique,
The happiness a void eliminated soon,
Writes out of the world completeness,
She grew up upbringing, I devote honestly,

Rejoiced her success learning well,
Her laughter, demand, complaints, fun,
Relished life of father noticed well,
Induced family culture, customs too,

Humble by nature, silent she preferred,
Her merit, talents like milk and water,
Pride could not touch her heart or ego,
Cooperative spirit, hardworking life,

Simplicity, her shield won hearts,
Admired, got applause, her degrees,
Advanced in life age browning effect,
The daughter grabbed a career job,

Her affluent life single years rolled on,
She got married outside of religion,
Did not inform her parents of her wedding,
When we heard about her marriage,

Socked me, and my wife, speechless,
How could she decide her life,
Unilateral her decision bypassed us,
Established us, unimportant, clearly,

Heartbroken, her mother cried a lot,
Strengthened me, self-assured,
Failed to digest the event accepted,
Look at my son, never given attachment,

He knew this sister got everything,
But fortunate we couple, he respects us,
Felt guilty, never demanded attention,
Well, his care, devotion, concern for us,

Never criticized his sister, not taking,
He got his job, respectable post, lucky,
We solemnized his marriage happily,
The day we received a daughter-in-law,

Beautiful, slim, voice soothing and kind,
Well qualified decides housewife life,
Stunned by her attentive care service,
The home changed soon to be a sweet abode,

Her behavior, culture, and graceful demeanor
Imprinted on our hearts her love and remark,
Watching her mother-in-law contented,
She praying for her daughter-in-law.

Once, I taunted her about our bride,
She looked at me, replied got a daughter,
My daughter-in-law is my daughter,
Till my last day, she is with me, my belief,

She is not that soul to betray us, my son,
Her divine stint in married life, beautiful,
She never expected loving parents-in-law,
The home amalgamated once devastated,

Inking my life, daughters are rivers, seemingly,
If a river breached embankment wrecked,
Other one flowing serenity matches paradise,
Daughters, if one denounced, other surprises.

Daydreams

Butterflies décor mind's garden,
Colors in spray, flowers gladden,
Thoughts as gentle breeze blow,
Sunlight, in a cool shade, mind glow,

Eyes lost in an unknown city bright,
Wide roads clean busy life in, sight,
Glass towers kiss blue sky high,
Homes of dwellers dazzle parks lie,

Thoughts as spider web grew more,
Train whistles speeding far allure,
Village life, quietude afternoon hours,
Young life results from success, idle sourness,

Nice flats, gleaming floor furniture,
Service life in city prime career,
Simple and serene village cottage,
Thatched roof, childhood craze,

Friends with wings high in the air,
Early marriages few missing n rare,
Village gossip, moonlit night distant,
A noisy evening with cake friends want,

Time has swallowed teenage, quick,
Village girl life behind door sick,
Education in school, college hostel,
Over time smooth in urban taste,

Cinema, bazaars, nightlife recall,
Shimmers daydream, window small,
No more village is beautiful, no jobs,
City life in scope, great future throb,

Mind misses among people strange,
Well dressed, with the busy time craze,
Dreams in crowded trains and buses quick,
Rushing office time looks evasive,

Mind swings joyful, office glamour,
Surprises in work tours often favor,
Few steps out of college life travel,
Metros, overseas trip, wonderfully unravel,

Colleague, handsome, friendly officer,
Dreamer dreams, ecstatic, life partner,
Mind a spider captures imaginations,
A residence flat, furniture, cushions,

Daydreams move ahead of a baby,
Lonely girl mid-afternoon dreams savvy,
Good is career, husband, baby, and home,
Amazing city life, family own awesome,

A knock on the door loud call disturb,
Daydreams fade soon, this heart perturb,
Opened the front door, and a postman with mail,
Anxious girl search, interview call detail,

Invitation as school teacher vacant,
Modest salary, quarter, a city as distant,
Mother queries daughter in a letter,
Marriage looms near, and fate tests greater.

Death Of Delusion

Saw great nations have big navies,
Saw countries with the deadliest armies,
Saw countries with nuclear missiles,
Saw countries with the best fighters,

Saw countries with satellite weapons,
Saw countries with many terrorists,
Saw countries with chemical weapons,
Saw countries with bio-weapons in the store,

They built this armada to secure a nation,
They cover the earth in base to spring invasion,
They terrorize weak nations,
Game of power, supremacy rule,

Convince their people to be safe, but a fool,
Delusions grasp people, feel supreme,
Make their dream empire in esteem,
Large healthcare nations boast,

At age, people celebrate life n toast,
A nation and its people are invincible, they think,
World at delusion, civilization never can sink,
A time came an unseen predator moved,

Nation to nation covered the globe,
By day people in thousands face death,
Only faces death out of breath,
It spread faster than the speed of the mind,

Entire gadget of weapons, an army of any kind,
Failed to neutralize the unseen terror,
Such a little microbe multiplies in horror,
No treatment health can afford,
The world got puzzled, thought it absurd,
Humans fight in the lab for cures n vaccination,
Illusion broke dawn on the death of delusion.....

Death Of Hypocrisy

Silent life, silent world, a canvas of serene nature,
Life grows in silence, ages live in grace, exist pure,
O' human, no new one, behold the tree fresh green,
Slow breeze play, get cool art, leaves shiver in gay,

Blazing a Sun, at the top, look below, the tree glisten,
Lost in the clue, transform a hot sand bed, cows listen,
Sweet murmur, leaves as fur, steal their innocent mind,
Purity exists, reject deceit, ill feelings unknown but kind,

Dry leaves are bed for animals, feed green leaves relaxed,
Cool shade brings sleep in grace, natural wonder a class,
So many cows stay in comfort, tree, look at the creator,
Fine divine, if you create, life passed serving soul other,

Never can speak, aware of around, cannot move ever,
Saw animals, birds, and creatures offer all as their home,
Never knows hatred, fear, cruelty, bias, sure none,
Knows leaves of life, fails to act, stays in guise on,

Name hypocrisy, never in service, a pretension,
Winter tree rejects dry leaves, bares branch,
Death of hypocrisy, spring green an avalanche,
New leaves show purity, serve the tree in love,

The tree shows humanity as a teen act like a dove,
Green is life purity and love, in heart, serve,
Tree or spirits near love their presence above,
Dare humans in guise stay pretends, dry on duty,

Sounds in a breeze, hypocrisy no use to be beauty,
The tree rejects, in a season, these leaves on the wind,
The great message, testing time, ever comes, unkind,
Suffering pain n measure, humanity cries a helping hand,

Hypocrisy in spirit loot exploit, exist as hot and dry sand,
Dry leaves cover the forest, never grow but decay n rot,
Permit fungi, and pest plenty, watch trees, decay frost,
Summer commences dry leaves torch fire a forest,

Grew from trees, see all perish in a fire to ash best,
Never dry leaves in pain in joy born, death is a wish,
Death is around, plants and animals exist as a curse finish,
Nature sends a message, humanity, hypocrisy, flourish,

Growth deter, parasites pest, home in their heart,
Spread fast, torch community, destructions so fast,
Watch in joy death prevail, same as a forest fire act,
Evil mind well in guise pretend to save born self,

As dry leaves go so fast, know hypocrisy never dies,
Green leaves times turn dry leaves and do fry,
Community do spread hypocrisy time n again,
The play enacted society's decay in ruins in vain,

Time watches, hypocrisy dies, new life so pure,
The creation of a proactive newborn in purity ensures,
Silent tree whispers life stories in wonderland!
Time, hypocrisy bites the dust, insane in the blade,
Death of hypocrisy purity is a Cool shade.

Deceit

Pretends life before Lord

Incredible human nature prays to God,
In happiness or sorrow, like a bud,
Grow in time overwhelm life in tears,
Heart pray to God on grace, in pain cure,
Tears are for self-joy, sadness as a sick,
Rare is a scene tear for other thick,
Rarest, the human spirit loves God, prays,
For destitute in a smile or hungry prey,
For orphans, street loners for shelter,
For dying slum dwellers in care swear,
Bestow on alter of the creator, own lifetime,
Deceit in dread for noble spirit in shine,
Prayer to self, joy or sorrow, to God earnest,
Divine love and deceit earn self-gain interest, (1)

Fake promises called sacred

Seven Vows couple commit witness fire,
Before Jesus admits couple tie nuts n share,
The ceremony is on divine oath for a lifetime,

Unite to walk in conjugal love outshine,
The share-of-joy n pain worries pleasure,
Trust faith in care serves mutual treasure,
Countless marriages, broken like glass,
The deceit smiles at both fire churches, awash,
Personal gain outlook rules over-promise divine,
Self-goals, greed, anger, hatred, cruelty, in time,
Lies deceit in the human heart's watch alert,
Weakest mind entrapped tempts till hurt, (2)

Joke in the name of God

The court of law called witness parties both,
All give due voice, in touch, in the name of God,
Address in court, they say, trust under oath,
Be it Bhagavata Gita or Holy Bible in law worth,
Hundreds of cases came to light later,
All lies are placed in court deceit on a platter,
Find an honorable court, trust oath to God,
Deceit rules in fake divine love a fraud,(3)

Betrayal in the name of faith

Watch leaders take an oath to serve the Constitution,
World imprint in the history of leaders of the nation,
From rags to riches, they grow in power,
People admire and applaud consent showers,
The oath starts, in the name of God as trust,
Constitution for people accepts God rules most,
Time project canvas of autocracy corruption,(4)

Glaring betrayal as the servitor

Deceit rules, nations use supreme in illusion,
In the name of our own God, deceit, prejudice, notion,
Crumple faith of people progress in erosion,
Crumbing honesty service to people in vision,
Deceit steals absolute power, ruthless, cruel,
Rat symbol of deceit filtrate grass-root swell,(5)

Broken professional integrity

An engineering doctor takes an oath to refuse corrupt,
Never surrender to rulers, integrity in jobs, lost,
The Alma Mater looks in tear, rotten, product,
How deceit creeps in ethics conscience inert, (6)

Fake followers of God

The cruel joke is deceit divine life manipulates,
Ages humanity love trust ascetic, communicate,
Shower with goods riches shelters in care,
Expect values clues in danger to save share,
In the guise of public faith, deceit, looting wealth,
Comfort luxury capture humans n breath,
Drug inquisitive mind as divine to taste,
Innocence cowers, surrenders, deceits, infests,
The temple of divine golden, most affluent,
The fight goes on, prayer, poor is needy insolvent,
Humans read Gita God dwells in the heart,
Idols abode misses Lord, deceit in rites art,(7)

Deceptive the realm

Nature deceit eons in creature landscape,
Quicksand is a hidden river plants precipice,
Ocean in water salty thirsty human cry,
Creature animals mimic leaves color shy,
Entrap, kill, or escape deceit plays here,
Cyberspace learns a honeycomb of innocent fear,
Hundreds of cookies trap information,
Customers in spider net leak information,
Money is a honey corporate fake honey bee,
All cash is stolen from digital cyber nets key, (viii)

Deceptive Human mind

The myth of deceit, never-ending, cast a spell,
Human life on the blue planet for eons dwell,
Deceits rule the human mind, slaves swell,
Who confronts and controls evil ring death knell.
Who conquers vanquishes, or deceit is a legend,
History read for a century in courage crescent. (9)

DECIDUOUS

How much astonished, stupefied,
The Barren land turns into a green field,
The pond-dried parched floor, lifeless,
To the brim, life manifested visibly,

The toads fish lotus bloom perennial,
Disappear summer heart surprising,
River flowing near our village serenely,
Skeletal serpentine sand bed blue stream,

Lo her swollen currents swirling water,
Gushing water foaming a hissing snake,
Lost her stamina, again placid water,
Full moonlight reflected stolen heart,

This is a river so exciting and beautiful,
Symbolize lovers den alluring embank,
Sails boatman his boat sings infect,
Local folksongs survive centuries,

Intoxicate night boating cool breeze,
The bride is leaving her parents wedded,
Crying the river, leaving a village girl she knew,
Moisten faces moisture-laden song,

Unknown home her to be abode,
She will be far from the river once bathed,
Returns father's home rive recognizes,
The waves greet her reflected glazing,

Sunlight above the river dazzles merrily,
Happy her daughter back reminisce,
Stood in my village, a tall banyan tree,
The square in narrow lanes attracts,

A platform around the tree memory,
Village people crowd at evening plays,
Gossip, their interaction, heated, socked,
Surprised mysterious rumors breed,

The decision of village head cases heard,
Looking at the tree deciduous leafless,
Lonely, a cement floor covered well,
Dry leaves have fallen tree intimate,

Wait, seasons rotate, green leaves blush,
Sway gently with gentle breeze whispers,
Announce other plants, foliage visible,
The mirth influences people to celebrate,

Flowering trees blossom color spread,
Fruit gardens with bud scented,
The barren land, wet raindrops play,
White music earth scent aroma infects,

Emotions floating, difficult to believe,
Speechless human life passes deciduous,
Dry lips cracked pale is the face,
Vacant look hunting silent shiver spine,

A thousand agonies suppressed a heart,
Still, frame motionless limbs stand,
Like a statue standing for hours with fewer replies,
Less explain her owes miseries and cruel fate,

Knew her very close shattered go,
Her child did not survive sickness cruel,
Broken her heart lost child a banyan tree,
Leafless branches missing the shed under,

The wind blows throw branches in horror,
Broken twigs fallen lifeless is time,
Her life resembles the tree melancholic,
Back home from city to village years after,

She ran towards me, greeted smiled,
Uncle, I have a son again, visit please,
I was searchingly looking at her,
Her long hair was shiny, flowing, wavy,

Black hair sounding her bright face,
Like the moon among dark clouds shine,
Her eyes were sparking gleefully,
Her bangles colored ere rings necklace,
She seemed a blossoming tree fragrant.

Delirious

Youth visits spirit was like a deer,
Restless, I was running madly,
Impatient to satiate curiosity running,
Brimming energy, able limbs,
Eyes alert, endless, insatiable hunger,
Mingling with people enjoying company,
Allure of fun, laughter, group song, dances,
Festive seasons celebrate mood travels,
Mirth is visible, noted the celebratory crowd, (a)

Forget pain, miseries, fever, hunger,
Effulgent happiness floods festival over,
Ears hooked to the occasion, memory stays,
Sang my life song of life felt pleasure,
Unlimited wanting heart small enough,
Throbbing, goaded rebelliously to be calm,
Running in the day at night disobeyed,
Never listened to elders searching my world,
Beautiful youth springing to challenge, (b)

Meet future plunder wealth at my will,
Wealth was my strength, health, vitality,
Successful in a study made life good,
Settled family life adulthood socking,
Never thought suffering these days a lot,
Sapping inner strength, diminishing energy, (c)

Weak, I got feverish, medicine failed,
Unknown disease bed, ridden delirious,
Blank mind thinks next dawn far,
Limbs trouble, cold, reasons failing,
Bedridden, dark in my room, light hurts,
Closed windows, air fail to tolerate, (d)

Thinking my youth, vitality superb,
Sickness stole my life, still stealing hope,
Desperately wait, night endless,
Absent sleep, worried, tensed mind,
What will happen tomorrow, ever recover?
May I see tomorrow's dawn sun rays?
Inhale fresh air lungful, watch healing,
Exertion, fatigue, tension culprit,
Sleeplessness, worried life, waiting for the end,
Culprit myself, not my fate or destiny, (e)

Ran for gold blindly, I ran, minted,
Hard work, the family lost me, now I think,
Workaholic, I shall get success,
Complete projects got applause, ovation,
Melted everything today into thin air,

Pleaded, my darling, to recluse soon,
Disclosed my wish to her, let me die,
Let me die amidst nature, I request,
Soul mingles with wind wilds gets freedom, (f)

Dreaming of greens, meadows, waterfalls,
Dreaming forest canopy of fog, thick,
Disappear within trees flowery,
Sleep on a velvet grass field, wildflower,
Colorful wildflower for a day fragrant,
Smiling and knowing tomorrow is too far,
Fallen flower, my spirit, matching, (g)

My beloved with me, in a wheelchair,
Kept my request, hill station here,
We are roaming within nature,
Miraculous recovery, healing silence,
Clean air, the freshness of life abundant,
Comparing me to a wildflower,
Delirious, unreal happiness overwhelms.
Delirious of the state in a dark room, forget,
I realized like never before. (h)

Delirium

Wondering in this big world hungry,
Wanting heart in askance torturous,
Tired limbs cover to sleep and never escape,
Dream takes over wanton desires,
Spread wings, curious, imagine endless,
Fame and fortune distant moon silvery,
Modest life from poverty life once originated,
God-given merit, nature industrious,
I adored the book the treasure in a Hamlet,
Feed floating dreams, treasure-seeking,
Studied burning midnight lamps, curious,
Couldn't satiate the thirst for knowledge,
Earth spins, nicely seasons rotate timely,
Abject misery couldn't deter aspirations,
A spring arrived, blossoming fragrant, in life,
Left obscure village to meet the challenge of fright, (1)

Fearful of an unknown world, saw viciousness,
Corners glittering, looking down upon have-nots,
Cruelty heartbreaking, life rich and educated,
Deceptions, visible in glittering houses,
Merciless hearts crowded bustling cities,

Exploiting weak, minting gold, untiring,
Flutters banner of freedom of civilized people,
Shaken, trembling inner fibers of the frame,
Speechless, I was standing on a road,
In the dead of night, searching for shelter,
The Vastness of the metropolis was empty,
Hunting senses in narrow lanes,
I could find shelter, and I slept,
Morning, it was different a world, picture,
Disbelieve the noise, crowd busy, running,
Time, O' time, too short for making money,
Build family, widen career, and amass wealth,
No respite, living dead with a flower, no tear,
Raised skyscrapers kissing the sky,
Glistening the towers, highways, travel,
Polished floors, bright walls of the interior,
Reflecting opulence, luxury, and comfort,
Behind the doors life, drinking power, lust, (2)

Shelter home free food, university degree,
Today achieved life, success in hand,
Money, social status, family, God's grace,
Lacks happiness, true love smiles in guise,
My intuition detects deception, anger rises,
Where is love, peace, my true nature?
I got in my teenage in sweet hamlet,
My city boasts outcries loudly pleasure plenty,
Immense to sensations yet lacking joy,
I knew experienced joy in the mountains, greens,
Experienced in blue River serpentine,

Lacking here life visibly seek, tense,
Quietude missing, silence rare sight,
No more a kid, education failed to give joy, (3)

Earth spins, another summer, so hot,
I returned to my village, my muddy home,
My family stayed in the city, here alone,
Villagers smiling at me, kids enquire,
Females offering homemade cakes, delicious,
The silence, darkness of the night, oil lamp,
I am resting got true happiness in delirium,
In delirium, I saw true love, life in joy,
My education fails to guide and find. (4)

Despicable

Incredible smiles of the baby catch attention,
Eyes glint, shiny amazes divine protection,
Innocence, pure a presence fizzle tension,
Attributes mature of a baby are absent,

The human mind erases despicable to decent,
Time passes, the life grows fast in a year,
Hunger, fun, fear infest, in pain cry, near,
The toddler walks, recognizes known faces,

Accustomed to calling names to talk in traces,
Anyone despicable is a jewel in teenage,
Innocence, love, fun, smile life essays,
Decades passed, human maturity knows clearly,

Good deeds, wrong things, feelings, endure,
Every action creates thought etches within,
Memories grow with events, human deeds shine,
Evil act escapades flutter thrilling heart,

Abstracts are feeling and guide the mind intact,
Love, care, serving all, helping others grow,
Kindness, humble nature, soft-spoken show,
A person gains praise, actions, and attitudes,

The same person can turn despicable in change,
Environment, friends, parents, media pollutes,
Society, community infects, decency dilutes,
Poverty, hunger, sickness, and broken homes lurk,

Richest, powerful, caste, blind faith often work,
A despicable leaves in every section in guise,
Evil feelings erase nobleness natures likewise,
Poisoned mind with attitudes, negative precise,

Hatred, greed, cruelty, lust intolerance are seen in plenty,
Anger unlimited plunders heartless property,
Destroys mindless in lust, vanity of female folk,
A people in pain, conscience silent, in shock,

Despicable nature often gets brutal, unprovoked,
A society least forgives retaliation stern revoked,
The name identity gets a black-painted image,
People tag it as a symbol of a despicable on stage,

The soul is never in sin, unaware of black deeds,
The purest one is attributed less, feelings cast or creeds,
Never humanity isolates the dark nature as the root,
Dignified, respectable, and mighty shrinks it to boot,

Passionately harboring these attributes commits a crime,
Escapes by wealth, and power, turns facts to favor the prime,
Eons human mind harbor divine or evil,
Noble suppress evil, despicable surrenders to the devil,

The soul departs spotless deeds follow with the mind,
Mind is scripted with attributes subtle to unwind,
Next life soul free of face, memories, despicable state,
Unwind dark deeds nature takes root hell-bent,

Infinite miseries and pain soul get for human nature,
Every humanity tramples within a wrong posture.
Despicable decimate in childhood disciplines,
Prayer, meditation, love, simple life, serene,

In silence, nature seclusion, divine life humility,
Caring for others and sharing happiness in life is noble,
Inner dark despicable temptations crumble,
Mind get firm in rail rolls mighty detached,

Every society on the path to gurukul, kids attached,
Gurukul is an ancient abode of knowledge,
Humanity gains divine natures in phases,
So powerful instinct of evil attitude within,

Weak moments, mind capture clean,
The fight between noble and despicable is visible,
Endless one, the only annihilation is a cure, simple,
God forgives a soul, punishes nature despicable,

Often incarnate to establish peaceful, secure,
God allows spirits to mend their ways,
God punishes unforgivable spirits to hell,
Traitors of people's trust, treason to the soil,

Predators of teen, female, oldest toil,
Stalkers with evil motives play as idol crushes,
Arsonists are on a rampage, people suffer, and worse,
System of rule discipline a beast crumple,
Protest recalls aggression assault simple,
Silence to macabre deeds wait in patience,
Despicable in time perishes, smiles innocence.

Devotion

The invincible power transcends humans,
Grace of Divine among Universe no one,
The power within humans is their minds n thoughts,
If in silence in the cavern, years a spirit is lost,

Sitting prostrate, breathing slowly, focusing on a point,
Abolish worldly bondage by the power of will,
No food, no water, but still on heat n cold on a hill,
Unaware of self-time n position concentration,

For a long, long time, intuitive within in dark prostrate,
The divine melt as one heart seeks revelation,
Grace many in ages power with devolution,
Indestructible existence acquires ego in greed,

Lust, blind anger entrap the soul, insidious it breeds,
Own inquisitive effort as such with a motive to gain,
Destroys one in time life lost all virtues in vain,
It happened among people on a minor scale,

One pursues knowledge and wisdom to get wealth well,
The same attitude gets insidious greed and cruelty in men,
Demons are called in ages got fear, now n then,
A spirit meant in divine path gets destroyed in lust,

Modern times renowned as decent in truth are worst,
The world today is civilized, with culture, name, and fame,
World n nature, destroyed, species but blame,
Divine creation at crossroads perturbed on mind,

Will power, penance, inquisitive intelligence find,
All were His gift are on-road to the extinction of the world,
Including their own race with bio-weapon if rewarded,
Lo' human, please listen to one word in our faith,

Be God, be Allah be Krishna aware in our breath,
Ultimate Divine Love, we acquire ever in us as a lesson,
All our sins, grave deeds that corrupt n torment,
Devotion finishes emotions, compassion gets fermented,

Kindness, love for nature, and earth, sympathy n care,
Hurt spirits, their pain agonies suffering we do share,
Only there is the path, divine blessing, forgive our sins,
The devotion of our life we offer in true spirit if, means,

Lord lacks only quality as He is ignorant of surrender,
None in creation He requires to worship better,
In mind in pure love and devotion merge with Lord,
Mother knew the Divine supreme world as absurd,

Once in love, Krishna touched the feet of Mother,
Devotions pleased Lord, Mother (Radha) in surrender,
This is the best use for times humans in confined,
Deadly viruses forced humanity home all time,

The right time to sit in devotion, love prayer, pray divine,
May Lord Graces us to usher wellness, nature will shine,
We are devoted deep, for mercy, Covid be gone,
Let the world get clean of virus life in blossom!!!
Message to the planet in pictures survive in extinction
Insidious inquisitive decimate in devotion,

Diaspora

The most ancient civilization persists,
Withstood the vagaries of time routed,
Stands till modern times look at twenty-first,
The century eagerly awaited stays supreme,

The triangle base of the Himalayas widest,
From the Hindukush to Rangoon expanse,
Touched the Indian ocean at Kanyakumari,
The peninsula of billion plus people plural,

Hosts countless cultures, tribes, ethnics,
Color the hundreds of languages, cultures,
The people believe in God's path numerous,
Citadel of interfaith tolerance coexistence,

Thousands of Masjids, Churches, temples,
Equal the monasteries education hubs,
All are growing majestic democracy help,
Freedom, fundamental right liberty won,

True equality for the vast population stark real,
Exercises franchise election mindboggling,
From destitute, laborer, and peasants to corporate,
From female, male, young or old alike,

Their index finger decides the ruler, mighty,
The opposite happens, massive landslides,
A tea seller child on a train gets victorious,
A newspaper boy minority is the president,

A tribal woman replaces his position,
Democracy, significant exercise, marvel,
The smooth transition of power progress,
Freedom to women, free education focus,

Senior citizens get support health onus,
Youth educated skilled migrate worldwide,
Ages ago traveled across the ocean as laborers,
Cane fields, granaries, industry demand,

Generations settled accepted nationalities,
The language, culture, food, dress styles,
Little eroded, still visible, the rituals,
Practices the same faith builds temples, Gurdwara,

Follows customs of forefathers practices,
Thousand miles away from ancestor's land,
Still, love treats the motherland feel nostalgic,
Remind centuries ago, traveled on ship,

Established built homeland children grew,
Flowing back home of forefathers, experience,
An ocean of life complex yet splendor pull,
Intoxicate festivals celebrate ancient land,

Smeared with colors spray color powder,
The dance song musical, drum rhythm,
Folk dancers dress in costumes, colorful,
The stepping ecstatic entices the heart to sing,

To dance in synch smiling soul is lost,
Tearful feels forefathers were like this,
Happy, prosperous, wise, knowledgeable,
Indomitable spirit, benevolent, kind, loving,

Hospitable, never been aggressor, gentle,
Knew, still recognize peace, care, compassion,
Love earth, nature, and the people of the world,
Brotherhood saves internal strife to amity,

Hundreds of islands in the ocean, countries,
Migration continues unabated, skilled,
Skilled people, now the spine of adopted land,
Engineers, doctors, scientists, builders,

Hardworking unscrupulous people,
Hiring respect, honor, rewards through work,
A few writers perform in art, culture,
World-class Diaspora linked to the past,

Travels very often visit length and breadth,
Experience millennia-old rich civilizations,
That extends a Diaspora over the globe.
Just one returned homeland freed from slavery,
In the third quarter of a century, indebted billions.

Diminishing Contour

The universe exists n amazes,
An expanse of unknown transfixes,
Merges mind in the night sky,
Million Sun, planet, moon lie, (1)

Invisible to physical sight, a say,
Doubt life stays distant dismay,
Milk way attracts n mysterious,
Who inhabits well, gets curious, (2)

The creator imposes vast creation,
The star moves to oblivion motion,
The contour of the existence probe,
Whose design merges with love, (3)

Love undefined play game best,
The diminishing contour quest,
Contours of living beings dwell,
Unknown planets, galaxy swell, (4)

Fails to grasp creation perplex,
Bewilder the master does flex,
Play cycles of birth-death n face,
Deathless a soul, sojourn I trace, (5)

Ends night contours of life think,
Creator, His purpose, heart sink,
Ponder within focus in darkness,
Witness a sight universe impress, (6)

Dark space, a void of silence n quiet,
Glimmer dim lights, sound duet,
Fails again me contours of space,
Resemble both, inner-outer grace, (7)

The aura, luminance, energy mist,
Discover within n earth ink in gist,
Menace of destruction, I astonish,
Demolish earthlings, nature miss, (viii)

Rebirth resurrection restarts well,
The river of time flows eternally quell,
Quell opposition, obstructions all,
Within the creator, enact cleanses roll, (9)

Infinite love and mercy purify matter,
Savagery anger the fire egos tatter,
Acts sun, moon, earth, mountain,
Like picture roll see love fountain, (10)

Capture thought war raises often,
Cruelty rules ruin life seen soften,
Softens, conscience bites evil deed,
Illness nature's wrath hits indeed, (11)

Convince wisdom action, reaction,
Human deeds mean little creation,
Virus, health disease-prone nature,
Human suffers that rises and pure, (12)

Eons humans discover death tools,
Puzzle wishes creator, nails fools,
Pandemic, epidemic sick life ruin,
Race, race to oblivion, divine clean, (13)

Watch inner nature, impure fight,
Battle of good nature n evil fright,
Replicate outer world looks exactly,
Defeat noble nature death, intact,
Human nature wins life safe enact, (14)

Creator plays life enacts in vain,
Wishes of the creator blindly claim, shame,
Actions of the Lord, pervade, enamor,
A self-deed is a diminishing contour. (15)

Discernible

At first sight, in life felt dumbstruck,
Surprised to disbelieve the monster moving,
Black smoke shoots in a gush,
Steam hissing out of wheels, horn,

Blaring, shaking me in fear,
Railway coaches, wooden chair rows,
Glass window big enough for view,
Travel on a train as a child etched,

Memory is a mixture of thrill, pleasure,
Rolling wheels in rhythmic noise,
Music to me at age floats sweetly,
Visiting summer vacation from school,

At maternal grandfather's house,
A hundred kilometers away from home,
Boarding morning train witness scene,
Running past slowly, villages and towns,

Crossing rivers iron bridge sound,
Middle of a forest, tearing mountain,
Vendors with a mixture of cake sweets,
Pleasant travel at an early age is memorable,

Grew up studying in a college far city,
Easier to travel by train journey restful,
Empty stations, few vendors shouting,
Fewer crowds watching the countryside best,

Poor villagers, suitcases, bags carrying,
Village products, wood for cooking,
Selling in the cities, they used to return to villages,
The train is their lifeline, picturesque attire,

Turban, dirty clothes, chapel, chew beetle,
Smoking near doors sitting on the floor,
Women with bangles vermilion on foreheads,
Shy, face covered with saree, sits aloof,

Gradually changing, people noticed,
Traveling on trains, shirts, pants, dresses,
Clean saree females freely mixing,
Talking on trains indulging in gossip,

Beetle, a constant friend, chewing a lot,
Children playing in the corridor smartly,
Coal engines no more diesel engines faster,
Wooden benches changed to cushions,

Longer the train, fast travel crowded,
Marked villages and towns, getting bigger,
Getting better, looking modern, traffic,
Vehicles, bikes, roads crowded, intersect,

Vanishing bullock carts, speeding cars,
Moving trains, I glued to landscape,
The country is now prosperous, populated,
Stations with shops, retiring room facility,

Cement benches, lighted at night, clean,
No more traveling in train twilight years,
Confined to home watching the news,
Bullet trains offing trains gleaming,

Faster travel, air-conditioned coaches,
Serving breakfast, lunch, and dinners on board,
Long distance travel a thousand miles,
Passing hundreds of station amenities,

Online booking travel got modern,
Million daily travel, business vacation,
Pilgrimage, studies, crowded station,
Coolies in red cloth badge peruse,

Carry baggage on the head, unload from a train,
Platform mile long, several platform links,
Life becomes complex, crowded, restless,
Running life trains day and night is noisy,

Mile-long bridge, tunnels, crisscross,
Weaving country spider web network,
After independence, travels phenomenal,
Seven decades after, I remember the difference,

Coal engine of my childhood, discernible,
Museum pieces at places of steam engines,
Reminisce, our land got freedom,
Cherishing iron cartwheels no more,
Generation metamorphoses, scenes, discernible.

DISCOLORED SKIES

Lamp lighten dark room feels comfort,
Fears stalk the mind fades instant effort,
Thought mischief monger create well,
Vogue horror hunt weaken heart nail, (1)

Darkness adds color opaque suspicion,
Predator prowls terrorize imagination,
The ultimate fear of death lurks exhibit neat,
Confusion cripples courage, hell excites, (2)

Close chamber windows shut create all,
Fresh winds light obstruct captive roll,
Deprive vibrant nature aroma of earth,
Life perish in dungeon customs worth, (3)

Imprisons female n domestic creatures,
Menial work grows children, live securely,
Behind curtains soul resists exposure,
Rule restriction break punish harsher, (4)

Close education higher school, college,
Colorful birds in cage food water craze,
Realities of modern society disbelieve all,
Equality of women at par with men tall, (5)

Beat male scholars in studies research,
Sport, career leadership quality search,
Female education skills exception often,
Industry corporate business life glisten, (6)

Ever such free birds thought to fly higher,
Colorful sky cloud performance glamor,
Nation feels proud female front runner,
Might of the nation womanhood secure, (7)

Army Navy air-force, spacecraft service,
No more restriction examples for novices,
Huge n free democratic nations prosper,
Brick of strength castle females secure, (viii)

Breeds quality life of children duly lead,
Fortify new generation conviction plead,
Bring notice ghastly dungeon exists well,
A million women linger rotten perish trail, (9)

Futile gathers the courage to protest practice,
Community segregates n boycott service,
Branded convicts commit sacrilege worst,
Family suffers, gets tortured, freedom cost, (10)

Close society even exists continents-wide,
Humanity does repent requests override,
Rarely, society reforms, freedom associate,
Liberation for womanhood ensures, relates, (11)

The lamp lightens, darkness recedes, fears fade,
Ocean of hope tidal wave tsunami invade,
Windows open, bright sunshine creeps nit,
Spread happiness desires colleges admit, (12)

Veils vanish, glint bright eyes spark wit,
Heartfelt laughter cherishes the nation explicitly,
Glamorous dress, ornate angelic figures all,
Happy bird fly gaily spell charms enthrall, (13)

Not at all fiction reality exist notion belies,
A bird in a cage cries silently, discolored skies.
Extinguishes candle of life smokes spread,
Discolor skies, dark smoke, spirits tirade. (14)

Discordance Dissipate

Dreamy springtime

Spring arrives in the garden,
Red rose smile miss burden,
Beautiful creeper its flowers,
Dews on grass glint showers,
Showers peace, happiness lot,
Youthful heart n limbs alert,
Rests drowsy mind's garden,
Endless dreams of life again, (1)

Spring of young life

Excellent in studies n career,
Name recognition to grow sheer,
Hard work n clean life are simple,
Impeccable character n single,
Middle-class tag fade, famous,
Influential personality copious,
Admiration, applause, success,
Charms, wife, kids, now impress, (2)

Spring is success

Bird chirps sweet awake mind,
Harsh life surrounds n rewind,
Rose petals miss dew dissipate,
Garden of life bleak hope wait,
Examination result hunt fear,
Success elusive lets pain tear,
Courage, patience, consoling self,
The effort, hard work, credits shelve, (3)

Spring dissipate discordance

Nightlong table lamp-lit books,
Intricate, complex, study hooks,
Dreams fade after long hour's labor,
Dawn breaks ready for exam hour,
Hours written test seem minute,
Satisfaction n results in fear of solute,
A week later, good news intimate,
Happy and discordance dissipate, (4)

Spring for job seeker

Discordance of mind reappears,
Again written test date, careers,
Future allures incredible service,
Tension anxiety failure precipice,
After months of practice and practice,

Exam-date arrives with little notice,
No answer to hard labor, fruitful,
Confidence and interview wonderful, (5)

Spring in married life

Excellent career wait for to dream,
Spring will return happiness brim,
The garden of the mind rose will blossom,
Aspirations ah... demand ransom,
Visualize enchanting lady invites,
Sure proposes her wedding vibes,
Modulate conjugal life build a home,
Happen fervent prayers blossom, (6)

Spring unite lovers

A sweet home, bitter truth, life test,
Break n make young hearts invest,
Result out, get the appointment letter,
Youthful mind discordant, better,
Posts girlfriend, welcome intimate,
Reads, then discordance dissipates. (7)

www.ingramcontent.com/pod-product-compliance
Lightning Source LLC
LaVergne TN
LVHW091615070526
838199LV00044B/807
9789356488915